WISDOM
WORKOUT

WISDOM WORKOUT

EXERCISE YOUR MIND!

RAJIV CHELLADURAI

Notion Press

Old No. 38, New No. 6
McNichols Road, Chetpet
Chennai - 600 031

First Published by Notion Press 2016
Copyright © Rajiv Chelladurai 2016
All Rights Reserved.

ISBN 978-1-946048-48-6

For Jenita, my warrior, my angel and my daughter…
I have learnt so much from you over the
last few months…

"In today's world, being yourself is a twenty-four hour job. Through these 'mental push-ups', Rajiv Chelladurai adroitly eggs the reader on to burn not calories but cobwebs in the mind, to convert stumbling blocks into stepping stones and to change what many construe as 'fate' with unshakeable faith - in ourselves."

Sanjay Pinto
Lawyer, Columnist, Author, Public Speaking Mentor &
Former Resident Editor - NDTV 24x7

"I have known Rajiv for over eight years now, and have always found him to be one of the most insightful people I have known. The book exemplifies that – focuses on the substance and separates it from the inconsequential. I loved the mental push-ups for the day – there is freshness to them, very distinct from the myriad of positive thinking quotes that inundate your FB and Twitter accounts today. Who would have thought that 'Sacrifice goes hand in hand with achievement? In order to grasp something you must be willing to let go of something else.' Outstanding!!!

But there is an element of humility and submission that coexists with achievement for it to be sustainable."

Raj Kamal
Global Head of Strategy and Corporate Development
(Investments, M&A)
Naspers Fintech-PayU at Naspers Limited

"It has been said that 'The unexamined life is not worth living.' This ancient saying is becoming increasingly relevant in the fast paced life that we live where we do not have time to pause and to ponder. Rajiv Chelladurai's book is meant to be a companion handbook for the journey of life. Familiar with the challenges of the corporate world and the struggles of life we all face, he provides us with a tool to help us to examine our lives, to ask questions, to reflect, to make the right choices and make positive changes that will enable us to enrich our lives and the lives of those around us."

Dr Sunil Abraham MBBS, DNB, DFM, FRACGP
Professor, Department of Family Medicine
Christian Medical College
Vellore, India

"There's wisdom to be found in not just reading but more so in living. There are plenty of books out there with so called "practical" wisdom tips written from a very universal perspective. What I find different in Rajiv's book - *Wisdom Workout* is that he shares his life's experiences in practical nuggets that can be applied by us who have similar experiences. The problem with life is that unlike in school, here we get the test first and then the lessons after. These lessons will be more lasting, but their cost is far dearer. If you can avoid heartache and disaster by reading about how others' poor choices brought such grief to them, so much the better. *Wisdom Workout* is one such book which offers those life's lessons with probing questions to enable the reader to reflect, internalise and practically apply it to his/her contexts and situations."

Anand Pillai
Design Thinking, Leadership
B2B Sales & Business Transformation Guru
Keynote & TEDx Speaker

"Wisdom Workout is a contemporary and refreshing inclusion to anyone's library. Rajiv Chelladurai, through his deeply searching questions and innovative format will ensure that you actually work with this book.

I have known Rajiv for the past few years and I must say that this workout is an autobiography of his walking the talk.

King Solomon is known as the wisest man on the earth. As a young man he had a dream where the Lord offered him riches, honour and wisdom. Solomon chose wisdom. Since he chose wisdom, the Lord gave him riches and honour and in addition, long life.

In my view riches are transitory; honour depends on others, while health and long life are gifts of God. Therefore, wisdom is the only thing which is innate and yours forever. Choose wisely and use the workout in your journey as a professional."

Emmanuel David,
Director, Tata Management Training Center

"Rajiv has distilled all his WISDOM into an easy to read, inspiring and uplifting book. If you are looking for a disciplined approach to become a master of your destiny, look no further, this is the right book for you. *Wisdom Workout* will challenge your intellect and mental push ups will build your myelin everyday…"

Rajan Kalia
Co-Founder of Salt Dee Fe Consultants

"Today's fast paced world has made connecting with yourself one of the most difficult tasks. Through Wisdom Workout, Rajiv offers the readers a way to cut through the clutter and gain mastery over the daily pressures to overachieve and the need to ascribe challenges and failures (more often than success) to others - people, circumstances and just plain fate. The book offers sincere advise, rationale and tools to take charge of your life and most importantly, devise a way to live in balance and happiness."

Rajesh Sud
Executive Vice Chairman & Managing Director
Max Life Insurance Co.Ltd

CONTENTS

FOREWORD

"In a world that is filled with busyness and humanity that is desperate for a quick-fix, there seem to be many remedies that are offered as solutions for whatever plagues us.

Occasionally amidst this chaos, there arises a voice of reason that cuts through the clutter with a methodology that returns ownership to the individual trying to change.

My good friend Rajiv has devoted his life to providing wisdom where knowledge ends and showing a path where the road seems to have disappeared. *Wisdom Workout* is one such compass for those seeking direction.

Written in a classic self-ownership format, this book is akin to going to a gym for the mind. It gives you the guidance and then asks you to complete the repetition while exercising a new thought and a new idea each day. Written for the amateur and the professional, this book and its learning continuum is a blue print for all walks of life. I am grateful to have been asked to offer a small endorsement and write the foreword for what I think is a revolutionary concept in the whole battle of skill and will. Where experts have given us the definitions of success and others have given us directions for achievement, this seminal work actually asks the individual to create their own game plan based on an assessment of assets and liabilities. I think the reader who is sincere with this approach to change will quickly find out that by learning 'why' any how will do."

Krish Dhanam
Author, *Hard Headed and Soft Hearted*
Global Ambassador for The Zig Ziglar Group & Global Adjunct for Ravi Zacharias International Ministries.

ACKNOWLEDGEMENTS

I would like to place on record my sincere thanks to my family who have been my constant inspiration and encouragement to make this book happen.

Christine Gershom and Rebecca Pearson have been involved with this project from scratch. Thank you for your time, effort and hard work. You guys are the best.

My mentors and friends who have chosen to endorse this book. You are people I look up to and it is a great honour to include your thoughts about this book.

Notion Press, thank you for agreeing to publish this book and for your support. You have been great to work with.

A BRIEF ABOUT *WISDOM WORKOUT*:

Wisdom Workout is the brain child of wisdom coach Rajiv Chelladurai who has envisioned it to be a daily guide to the practical application of wisdom. The book is structured in such a way that it contains brief thoughts penned by Rajiv on each page followed by an interactive 'workout' which is basically an invitation for the reader to get involved with the thought and interact with it by penning down how they will practically apply it to their contexts and situations.

The 'workout' process includes a set of questions based on Rajiv's thoughts that are crafted with intent to get the readers thinking, re-thinking and getting hands-on with the rational execution of the thoughts in their life. The book will challenge, push and exhort the reader to strive for excellence in their personal and professional lives.

WHO IS THIS BOOK MEANT FOR?

A professional seeking to set himself apart, an artist looking to distinguish himself, a housewife seeking clarity of her purpose, someone who is unemployed and seeking direction, a student who hasn't decided their life goals, an entrepreneur looking for inspiration or anyone who wants to work towards achieving success in whatever they do. This book is a wisdom coach to anyone seeking to set themselves apart by striving for excellence through practical application of wisdom. Anyone with a desire to grow and a willingness to learn qualifies to use this book.

HOW TO USE WISDOM WORKOUT

Life can be busy but it is futile to be busy minus being wise. Commit a minimum of ten minutes daily, preferably in the morning before you begin your day, to get 'coached'. Begin your training by reading Rajiv's quote on a page, dwell on it and answer the questions below. By doing so, you will internalise the learning and cause yourself to apply the same.

It is recommended that you pause once a week to rewind and reflect on your learnings and more importantly its applications.

Don't read this book like you read any other book. In fact, don't read this book at all. Use it like a mental dumbbell — at your own pace, consciously exercising your wisdom muscles daily.

This book is your personal wisdom development tool and each reader needs his or her own copy. It will help someone who hears you talk about the benefits of the book as much as it helps one lose weight just by hearing someone else's gym stories.

Here are some important things to note before you start using *Wisdom Workout*:

1. **This is not a book.** That's right. *Wisdom Workout* is not leisure reading. It is not a coffee table book. It is definitely not a thriller novel that you can't put down. In fact, you will want to put it down several times…

usually when you are writing in it! This book is meant to be used as a personal coach that will help you progress on your journey towards effectiveness in wisdom. However, how successful a coach the book will be partly depends on you, which brings us to the next point, honesty.

2. **Truth or Dare or Both.** You have a choice — answer questions on each page superficially and in a jiffy or take your time and be brutally honest. The former won't help much but with the latter approach you will find yourself thinking more, writing more, and of course, learning more. Dare to pen down your thoughts with complete sincerity!

3. **Scribble, doodle, and draw.** Regard Rajiv's ideas on each page as thought catalysts. Go beyond answering the questions below them. Write down other thoughts that you have regarding the topic. Talk about them to your mentor, a friend or just about anyone who you feel like discussing it with. Make sure you are open to learn and more importantly open to change the way you think. Use colourful post-its, if necessary, to mark pages that are important to you. Revisit them. It's alright if your book looks messy; you won't be messy when you are done with it!

4. **Take your time.** Don't rush through the book. If you can do one page a day, great! If you want to do one page a week, that's okay too! Find your pace but keep moving forward. Find a buddy or a group of friends who want to embark on a similar journey with you and make this a group experience. Ask each of them to get a book and meet them periodically to discuss

your progress. Accountability is a good thing and it will help you grow.

5. **Have fun.** This book isn't meant to make you a square. Being wise doesn't mean having a long face and an even longer beard as many Hollywood movies have portrayed it. Wisdom is growing to be a more effective person over time and doing that without having a good time on your journey isn't an option! Find ways to make this experience life-changing and enjoyable at the same time!

A NOTE FROM THE AUTHOR

Understanding the difference between *wisdom* and *knowledge* is a prerequisite to using this book. People who possess a wealth of *knowledge* aren't always 'wise'. That's why being able to distinguish the difference is what will set you up to use this 'Wisdom Coach' in the best possible way.

Knowledge is about know how while *wisdom* is about insight, discernment and application.

One may have *knowledge* but not *wisdom* but if one possesses *wisdom* he or she would also possess *knowledge* and understanding.

Knowledge is necessary but *wisdom* is mandatory to excel and live an honourable and satisfied life.

All things being equal among two individuals — be it education, upbringing, talent and opportunities — the one who practices *wisdom* is the one who is destined to get ahead. *Wisdom* is the X-factor. Like anything precious and valuable, it needs to be desired and pursued.

My conviction is that no one is born with developed *wisdom* but one need to make a conscious and regular effort to develop it.

High IQ levels are helpful but a man or woman who practices *wisdom* can be stopped by none. It dwells in the mind and heart of a person.

Wisdom is like a muscle which needs to be worked on daily. Its development requires daily exercise and a diet which supplements and aids it. If no exercise and careless intake of unhealthy food results in an unhealthy physical body that is prone to various kinds of ailments; similar is the case with a mind that is devoid of proper nourishment and exercise. Such a person ends up making poor choices, decisions and more importantly loses their sense of purpose.

The most critical aspect of *wisdom* is its application. This is the most significant differentiation —*knowledge* 'knows' but *wisdom* 'does.'

Wisdom won't just show up at your door step, you have got to desire it, pursue it and be willing to make significant trade-offs to acquire it.

It will cause you to:

✓ Be great at maintaining and building relationships

✓ Be a person of integrity

✓ Choose well and make the right decision

✓ Be a great leader

✓ Be a problem solver

✓ Manage your resources, time and money well

✓ Become a person who can be counted on

✓ Develop credibility and a trustworthy reputation

If you walk in *wisdom* consistently…

✓ People with power and authority will solicit your advice

✓ When you speak, others will listen intently

✓ You will live a life of purpose and leave a legacy

Here are some examples of the difference between *knowledge* and *wisdom*:

✓ *Knowledge* is being aware that smoking is injurious to health but it is *wisdom* that enables you to act on this *knowledge* and decide to avoid smoking.

✓ *Knowledge* is being aware about the importance of physical exercise but it is *wisdom* that causes you to decide to eat healthy and to be disciplined to stick to an exercise regime.

✓ *Knowledge* tells you to work hard for the family but it is *wisdom* that makes you realise that the most precious gift you could possibly give your family is your time.

✓ *Knowledge* could cause you to react to a situation based on past experience but *wisdom* will cause you to respond well with the future in mind.

This book promises to give you an excellent *Wisdom Workout* daily. I hope that now the word *'wisdom'* is put in proper perspective.

WISDOM IN CHARACTER

I chose to begin my book speaking about character as that is literally the building block of our lives. Everything we do or say or grow into stems from what our character is about. My character was shaped primarily by something I would have never chosen for myself, adversity. At the age of nine, I lost my mother to terribly tragic circumstances. Losing her was by far the greatest loss in my life as I lost a friend, a confidante, an encourager and a source of great love and care. Growing up with mom around was great as I was excelling in my studies and had huge dreams about everything that I wanted to accomplish. But here I was, alone all of a sudden, bereft and forced into circumstances that I had never foreseen. My grief and loneliness led to a very premature addiction to alcohol and a series of wrong relationships. I was always on the lookout for a relationship that would make up for the loss of my mom and that would make me feel loved and accepted as only she could. Sadly, my life only went downhill from there. My addictions took charge of my life and threatened to pull me under unless I did something and fast. As I turned eighteen I looked back on my life so far and found, to my utter dismay, not much to go on for. I contemplated and attempted suicide a couple of times and, to my chagrin, was unsuccessful in my attempts. I then realised that my life had to count for something. There had to be more than what met the eye.

I decided I needed to whip my life back into shape if I wanted to achieve those dreams that I had dreamt for myself when mom was around. During this time a teacher from school took me under her wing and went way beyond her call of duty and mentored me. After school, tuition classes became treasured times of values being instilled in me that have stood me in good stead. Ms. Audrey Satur holds a special place in my heart for taking time to invest into my life and shape me into the man that I am today. But the crucial link to developing my character and shaping it was and still is my spirituality. Born in a strong Christian home, prayer and reading of God's word had been instilled in me from a very young age. As I grew, reading the Bible was more habitual than anything else. Thankfully this was one habit that changed my life and for the better. Promises like "I will never leave you nor forsake you" catered to my wounded, grief stricken spirit. The command to "Do everything as unto God" taught me my work ethics and the directive, "be humble", changed my attitude in relationships. In short the Bible was my safety net! Where would I have been without the powerful Word of God?

GREAT CHARACTER DOESN'T COME EASY THOUGH.

Like everything of value it comes at a price and often with much sacrifice. I discovered the price to develop good character was to let go of certain things and embrace others. For one, I had to let go of certain relationships which were dragging me down. It was a tough call to make since these were friends I had shared a big part of my life with. But having my cake and eating it too was not an option anymore. I therefore made a clean break from the relationships that had long since derailed me from my purpose. I had to also let go of my addiction, which was, let's face it, not heading me in the right direction. I realised that I drank if I was happy, sad, alone or with company. Nothing mattered as long as I had a drink in my hand or so I thought. But the more I considered it, the more I realised that I had lost the ability to make correct choices and to think rationally. Nothing, and I mean nothing, was worth that. Once I tossed the habit there was no looking back but there were a few things that I had to consciously embrace. I needed accountability and so came in mentors and friends and later on my spouse who have kept me accountable and in check. I also needed to begin to use talents and gifts that were inherently in me. I knew I could speak, teach and write so I had to stop shying away from opportunities to use those talents. I also began to teach young people from the lessons I had learnt in my life and found that it helped many. I actively pursued my gifts to fine tune them and make them sharpened instruments in my tool belt.

CHARACTER IS NOT WHO WE ARE IN PUBLIC BUT WHO WE ARE IN PRIVATE.

I'm a strong believer of the fact that private choices affect public persona and eventually public performance. I remember, in my previous assignment at work, the project that I was working on, gave me a fuel allowance of Rs. 20,000 for a month (Rs. 2.4 lakhs a year) which would give me a tax exemption. This was a huge amount as in reality I only used around Rs.5000 per month. Colleagues at work would routinely, at the end of the financial year, go to the different petrol stations and pick up random fuel bills to somehow account for their Rs. 20,000 allowance. I decided early on in my career that integrity would guide my every decision. So I ended up claiming an annual amount of just about Rs. 60,000 and wound up paying tax of Rs. 54,000 for the balance 1.8 lakhs. In spite of the sneers and jeers of my friends and peers I felt a great sense of peace and satisfaction at my actions. From personal experience I can confidently say that a life of integrity is marked by increased responsibility and greater access to people in authority. It also causes them to confide in us as they find us trustworthy.

THE BATTLE FOR GOOD CHARACTER IS MOST OFTEN IN THE MIND.

The human mind is our lifetime's treasure so I believe that we must do all that we can to develop a healthy and sound mind. Develop the mind? You might ask me isn't our mind just what it is? Well, I have found that the mind is like a muscle. And just like any muscle in the body that you want to build or tone it has to be, on a daily basis, strengthened and stretched in order for results to be seen. So also the mind, in order to be healthy, has to on a daily basis be renewed so that all the old, unhealthy thoughts are pushed out and fresh, healthy and positive ideas are pumped in. Just like the necessity to launder our clothes and shower everyday it is absolutely essential for us to renew our thoughts every day for a vibrant and nourished mind.

Very often our thoughts become *mindsets* and can hold us back from accomplishing all that we are meant to accomplish.

VICTIM TO VICTOR - IT'S ALL IN THE MIND

When things don't go as we hoped we tend to get into a victim *mindset*. But the challenge is in making the best of any given situation and coming out of it with a victor *mindset*. I previously worked in a prominent sales role with responsibility for a large geography of three states. Out of the blue, thanks to an organisation shuffle I was given a new role in innovation and sales automation. This new role was completely new to me since it didn't involve my area of core competence which was sales and which had no precedence in the company. It would require a lot of pioneering work for me to even make a dent. Friends and co-workers felt I got a raw deal and frankly so did I. But the choice was entirely up to me as to whether I was going to act like a victim or to make it work and make it big. Considering I had no background in this field I had very few ideas as to how to do sales in a novel modern way as opposed to the traditional approach. I led a team that introduced technology to encourage mobility and additionally put together interesting and intelligent applications to help people at the point of sale. The application was recognised and awarded the Celent model insurer Asia award, one of the leading IT bodies that recognise innovation. This was a result of the shift. A decision to make the most of any situation without falling prey to the victim mentality. This helped in moving me from having experience into the vast area of distribution technology. A victor *mindset* sets us on a path of newer opportunities, richer experiences and greater achievements.

RENEWING THE MIND IS ALL- IMPORTANT

The renewing of our mind is crucial to our success in life since it has the potential to make or break us. I know this to be true for a fact, because as I stepped out of my addiction I had many chances to slip back into old ways. But I had to speak to my mind every morning telling myself about everything that I could accomplish if I was alcohol free and lucid. It also helped that I was physically fit and healthy compared to when I was under the influence. Good company and habits are great starts to cultivating a healthy mind. I advocate reading at least ten pages of a book every day to inculcate a sound mind. It might sound funny to you that I spoke to my mind but those few months of conditioning my mind and disciplining it shaped my mind forever. Any thoughts that would threaten to damage my resolve or send me spiralling downward were instantly disallowed. I had to fence my mind in to protect it from damaging thoughts and attitudes and set a mental door in front of it which I carefully monitored through the things I watched, listened to and got involved in. You wouldn't build a house and leave it wide open for terrorists, bandits and armed robbers to enter and steal you blind would you? I didn't think so. Then why should we allow negative emotions like fear, worry, depression and insecurity find their way into our minds. Let's guard our mind with all vigilance! It's our treasure!

Thoughts are akin to currency. You could either create a profit or loss, either create a legacy or destroy character depending on the quality of your thoughts. Thoughts determine every facet of our life, be it health, career, finances, relationships. Thoughts determine our destiny. Thoughts need to be evaluated on a daily basis in order to keep them in check. Feed the mind with a nutritious thought meal, eliminate toxic thought patterns, disassociate with people who generate wrong thoughts and discipline yourself to think the right thoughts. Remember you speak to yourself way more than others speak to you so make sure you speak the right thoughts to yourself.

CHARACTER VERSUS CAREER

Knowledge, skill and talent are definitely important for a great career.

But their benefits are nullified in the absence of character. Many super talented corporate honchos, sport stars and artists have fallen by the wayside due to an appalling lack of character. Character is the glue that holds values in victories, integrity in ambition, right choices with consequences and values people more than performance. Character will sustain you over the long run. It is the raw material that helps you build a legacy. After over two decades of working in the corporate sector I can say confidently that character never hampers productivity. It has on the other hand only enhanced it. Performance will be applauded but character will be celebrated.

REPUTATION VERSUS RELATIONSHIPS

Relationships matter significantly more than reputation. One of the greatest treasures we have is our relationships. Reputations are what we aspire for others to think about us while character is what we know about ourselves. Strong and meaningful relationships require strong character. The thing with reputation is that it's more of an external attribute while character is entirely internal. Since reputation is primarily external it can be altered and manipulated to suit people, occasions and conditions. In addition, it being external, it involves our ego. Character on the other hand, being internal cannot be altered with. We can for a short time try and project a version of ourselves to the world but what goes on internally can't be played with. We know exactly who and what we are so we can't fool ourselves. The DNA of character is credibility. The bedrock for satisfying and lasting relationships is credibility. When credibility is lacking our relationships leak and ultimately break. Relationships require partners or participants to be vulnerable with each other. This is where altered reputations get exposed. Character and credibility stand consistent across the passage of time.

VALUES VERSUS VALUABLE

Wisdom enables us to tell the difference between the two and discern what true valuables are. We often place value on events and issues which in the larger scheme of things don't matter. I once heard of this quote of how "No one on their death bed has ever said that they wish they had spent more time at work."

Most people on their death beds have had regrets that they didn't spend time with their spouse and children. The cliché is really true of how many spend all their health to gain wealth and then in the latter part of their life spend all their wealth to regain health. In today's age where the mantra is "survival of the fittest" and self-worth is the designation printed on the visiting card, valuables seem to be achievement or profit. We live as if tomorrow is guaranteed when in reality it is absolutely not. What if hypothetically today is my last day on earth? I would spend it primarily with my wife and kids, listening to her and playing with them. I would also want to set my relationship with God right following which I would attempt to make right, relationships with old acquaintances if they had, at some point, gotten sour due to negligence on my part. I would find opportunities to bless those in my life who I could and I would laugh a whole lot more. These for me, are my true valuables. If you notice, my list did not involve crying over a missed promotion or accumulation of wealth or building a business empire. You get one shot to live life. Live well! Distinguish early on what your true valuables are.

CHARACTER MEANS STAYING GROUNDED AND NOT FLYING UNREASONABLY HIGH

Rudyard Kipling so aptly said in his poem *If*, "If you can meet with triumph and with disaster and treat those two impostors just the same you've done well."

What he means in simple words is not to get carried away by victory and to not lose sleep over defeat. I've come to understand that the journey of life comprises of both mountain top experiences and valley moments. Neither of them is a permanent destination. Neither lasts forever. One should exercise far more caution when dealing with a victory than when faced with defeat. In my mind, I'm convinced that pride precedes a fall and humility precedes a promotion. Therefore, handling victories should be done wisely. I would be lying if I say that a win doesn't bring me happiness because a victory is a culmination of effort, persistence, planning and execution. But the truth of the matter is that life moves on and the win will finally be only a distant memory. Failure is, at worst, a missed opportunity and at best, a learning tool. Never forget that the greatest inventions didn't happen on a first attempt basis but were the result of several failures. At a higher level, to be satisfied is superior to being happy. Satisfaction is almost always others-centric. For me to see my efforts have resulted in others succeeding, growing or being blessed gives me immense satisfaction. What keeps me grounded is the fact that people will forget my victories but they will always remember my assistance, support and availability for them when in need.

GREAT STEWARDSHIP IS AN OUTWORKING OF GREAT CHARACTER

Stewardship is the manner in which an individual undertakes a specific responsibility given to him or her as if they own it, given the fact that the ownership really lies with someone else. Trust and dependability is built when one practices stewardship. For me, stewardship is never judged by the quantity managed. When one is faithful with little and demonstrates stewardship in that, only then will they be entrusted much. We all want big breaks, the big opportunity but unless we prove to be trustworthy of the little, we will not get it. Stewardship is operational with little or no supervision. Stewardship and supervision do not co-exist. It's a character that causes excellence even in the absence of any monitoring. Stewardship also presents equal opportunity to all. For instance, a student preparing for his studies without being coerced and prodded to do so exhibits stewardship or a junior level executive doing way more than asked because he realises his every effort counts in the bigger scheme of things, the welfare and success of the organisation. A home maker avoids wastage and helps in saving much for her family causing the family as a whole to be benefitted.

Stewardship requires the making of right choices. One cannot afford to make poor choices and be a good steward. An employee who consistently arrives late at work or who procrastinates work cannot be considered a good steward. On the other hand, if an employee completes work ahead of the team and also initiates tasks that were not explicitly mentioned is considered proactive. Stewardship involves excellence and not existence. Doing tasks consistently and doing them well are considered traits of stewardship. The norm today is to do just what is asked and not more. The justification for this attitude is that this is all I have been paid for so why do more. But that is not the attitude of a good steward. He or she is willing to do even the mundane consistently and proactively. This positive attitude and ethic will definitely be noticed and will, in the long run, be rewarded.

I urge you to practice stewardship as stewardship will open doors to elevation.

Mental Push-Up for Today:

"Oh Yes! Life is unfair…but complaining, blaming others and wallowing in self-pity won't make it better. A positive attitude, specific goals and clear cut action will."

How do you react when you feel you are being treated 'unfairly?'

_____

_____

_____

_____

What personal steps can you take to having a more positive attitude today?

_____

_____

_____

_____

What are some specific goals that you can set and clear cut action that you can take to overcoming your frustration of 'feeling that life is unfair?'

_____

_____

_____

_____

_____

Mental Push-Up for Today:

"At the end of the day, character will matter more than career, relationships more than reputation, a life of purpose more than property and values more than valuables. Wisdom is to recognise this truth now rather than to realise it when it is too late."

Character vs. Career: Your CV normally has a 'career objective.' Write down a 'character objective' here.

_____

_____

Relationships vs. Reputation: Does getting more likes on your Facebook account count more than spending more time with friends and family? Write down how much time each week, you spend on social media vis-à-vis real conversations with people.

_____

_____

_____

Purpose vs. Property: Do you day-dream more about fulfilling your life purpose or living a wealthy lifestyle? Remind yourself of your life purpose by writing it down here.

_____

_____

_____

_____

Values vs. Valuables: What are some values you hold more important than possessions?

_____

_____

_____

_____

_____

_____

_____

_____

_____

_____

_____

_____

_____

_____

_____

_____

_____

_____

_____

_____

Mental Push-Up for Today:

"The true measure of greatness is the ability to stay grounded when you feel at the top of the world."

Make a note of your achievements or successes that make you most proud.

_____

_____

_____

_____

_____

Recall the struggles you faced to achieve the above and take a moment to "thank God" for helping you get there.

_____

_____

_____

_____

_____

_____

_____

_____

_____

_____

Mental Push-Up for Today:

"Medical studies prove that those who choose to be thankful live healthier lives versus those who constantly complain or are consistently dissatisfied."

Today, make a note of all the things you are thankful to God for — small and big. Write down as many things you can think of.

_____

_____

_____

_____

_____

_____

_____

_____

_____

_____

_____

_____

_____

_____

_____

_____

Mental Push-Up for Today:

"Working on your strengths will cause you to be far more effective than trying to fix your weakness."

List your strengths in detail here. Don't be modest and write down every one of them!

_____

_____

_____

_____

_____

_____

_____

How many of these strengths do you use every day? How can you work on the ones that aren't really being tapped into?

_____

_____

_____

_____

_____

_____

_____

_____

Mental Push-Up for Today:

"The quality of your thoughts determines the quality of your life."

Proverbs 23:7 – "For as he thinks in his heart, so is he."

Honesty Zone: Time to examine the health of your thought life…

Would you call your thought life:

a) Extremely Healthy   b) Moderately Healthy

c) Mostly Unhealthy   d) Extremely Unhealthy

Now, in detail, justify your choice of response with today's Push-Up in perspective.

_____

_____

_____

_____

_____

_____

_____

_____

_____

_____

_____

_____

Mental Push-Up for Today:

"I believe that God is most impressed with our right choices and conduct when we are alone. The test that leads to promotion is at the location of solitude."

Take a moment to let this thought sink in. Now, write down how you can apply it to your situation and what thoughts come to your mind immediately.

_____

_____

_____

_____

_____

_____

_____

_____

_____

_____

_____

_____

_____

_____

_____

Mental Push-Up for Today:

"Credibility is not what you preach or what you portray before others, it is simply about ensuring your *Yes* is a *Yes* and your *No* is a *No*!"

Honesty Zone: When you say *Yes* to something or someone, can you be relied on to keep your word? Write down your thoughts here.

_____

_____

_____

_____

_____

_____

_____

Now, what practical steps can you take towards being a more credible person?

_____

_____

_____

_____

_____

_____

_____

Mental Push-Up for Today:

"The outcomes we experience in life are a consequence of what we allow our minds to dwell on."

Flex your mind muscles. Think back through the past month. What has made up the content of your thoughts? Describe the themes below in brief.

_____

_____

_____

_____

Now, what outcomes have occurred in the past month directly related to these thoughts? Write them down and you'll notice a pattern.

_____

_____

_____

_____

What kind of outcomes do you desire to see in the coming month and what thoughts can you choose to dwell on to experience those results?

_____

_____

_____

_____

Mental Push-Up for Today:

"To take care of the body is important but to take care of the mind is critical. Mental strength will outlast physical strength."

Honesty Zone: In recent times, have you had a chance to exhibit mental strength? If Yes, when?

_____

_____

_____

_____

_____

_____

_____

Do you regularly keep a check on your mind so that thoughts and attitudes are not causing any unhealthy behaviours or thought patterns? If not, how can you plan to do so regularly?

_____

_____

_____

_____

_____

_____

_____

Mental Push-Up for Today:

"The art of 'joyful living' involves being content in every situation, finding reasons to be thankful in every circumstance and making the best of every opportunity."

Honesty Zone: Would you call yourself 'joyful' and 'thankful'? Give reasons for your response.

_____

_____

_____

_____

_____

_____

Make note of things in your life at this current moment that make you joyful and that you are thankful for.

_____

_____

_____

_____

_____

_____

Mental Push-Up for Today:

"Footholds graduate to strongholds beware! Addictions don't form overnight they develop gradually through actions which have been permitted a foothold and which eventually become a stronghold, controlling and destroying every area of life."

Time to introspect. Are there things in your life right now that you seem to be getting addicted to? Make note of them below. It could be something as seemingly harmless as texting or social media or spending frivolously.

_____

_____

_____

These seemingly harmless activities or habits can easily become your downfall. How you plan to ensure that they don't? Do you have a way to curb your attachment to this activity?

_____

_____

_____

Do you have someone in your life you can be accountable to with these things? If so, write their name here. Ensure that you speak to them to hold you accountable to your journey of overcoming.

_____

_____

Mental Push-Up for Today:

"Never come to a conclusion before ascertaining all the facts."

Think of a controversial matter in your gamut of influence that needs your attention to be resolved? Now, note down the different people you can talk to, the several sides of the story you must consider and make a detailed list of all the possible angles you must consider. Write them down here. This is just an exercise to help you understand how often you can miss out on certain aspects of a situation by just not considering them.

_____

_____

_____

_____

_____

_____

_____

_____

_____

_____

_____

_____

_____

Mental Push-Up for Today:

"Credibility outweighs popularity. It is better to be respected by few than to be liked by all.

Do you have some character goals where credibility is concerned? How can you seek to earn credibility by building specific aspects of your character in the next few months?

_____

_____

_____

_____

_____

_____

Here's something else to think about: Do you consider yourself to be someone who seeks to be "liked by all" or "respected by a few?" Either way, why do you think that is?

_____

_____

_____

_____

_____

_____

_____

Mental Push-Up for Today:

"Pride leads to arrogance which in turn leads to a false sense of invincibility which leads to a dead conscience, resulting in poor choices which culminate in moral failure and disastrous consequences."

Write down how you think pride can enter your life specifically. What are the ways in which you can avoid it?

_____

_____

_____

_____

_____

_____

_____

_____

_____

_____

_____

_____

_____

_____

_____

Mental Push-Up for Today:

"The true measure of greatness is the ability to stay grounded when you feel at the top of the world."

When you encounter success how can you ensure that you stay grounded and humble? Write down your thoughts on this.

_____

_____

_____

_____

_____

_____

What are some honest challenges you face where humility is concerned if there are any?

_____

_____

_____

_____

_____

_____

_____

Mental Push-Up for Today:

"One's response to stewardship will either culminate in promotion or demotion."

Stewardship can be best defined as being responsible for managing what has been assigned to you in an accountable way.

With this in mind, do you feel that you are a good steward of everything that is under your area of responsibility? Respond honestly and justify your response.

_____

_____

_____

_____

_____

_____

What are some honest challenges you face where humility is concerned, if there are any?

_____

_____

_____

_____

_____

_____

_____

Mental Push-Up for Today:

"Expect the best and stop expecting the worst, because you often get what you expect."

Do you consider yourself to be a positive person where expectations are concerned? In any situation, what do you normally expect – the best or the worst?

_____

_____

_____

_____

_____

_____

Write down some positive expectations that you have from the year ahead. Don't worry about them being unrealistic or not, just write down what your expectations are.

_____

_____

_____

_____

_____

_____

Mental Push-Up for Today:

"Choose to live with a mindset of a victor and not a victim.
You cannot choose both, your mindset of a victor or a victim
will determine your outcomes."

Is there a situation in your life right now where you feel like a
victim? Write about your experience here.

_____

_____

_____

_____

_____

What exactly can you change about your mindset that can
make you feel like a victor in this same situation?

_____

_____

_____

_____

_____

_____

_____

WISDOM IN PURPOSE

A person who lives out his or her purpose is one who has a vision of the larger picture and is driven by a larger cause. Such a person has gone beyond the sphere of career and is living out their calling.

I believe my personal purpose is to inspire others and I will inspire through speaking, writing books and leveraging social media. I really believe that as a society, we continue to make progress and grow financially but there's an ever- present need for inspiration which somehow goes unattended. Depression is one of the fastest growing epidemics of our time. I stumbled upon my purpose when personally going through periods of down times laced with suicidal tendencies. While the need to inspire and be inspired is obvious, it really isn't all that apparent. Having had the good fortune of having learnt from my own experience and also to inspire people within my circle of influence and see them benefit from it, I realised that the process and outcome of inspiring others made me feel complete. I recognised, not wanting to sound proud here, that I could inspire others around me. Like a light bulb going off it dawned on me that this was my purpose. I have had, over the course of time, the opportunity to live out my purpose in inspiring others in various settings and geographies. I have also used social media to inspire a larger audience. It has been thoroughly satisfying but I have had to make many sacrifices, especially with managing time. It is critical that when you want to inspire others you are available and that you are inspiration worthy. Which means that you are prepared, positive, excited and you have a constant supply of fresh, relevant and energizing content. You have to be able to inspire people with advice that you have applied in your life personally. For instance, I have always been an advocate of a healthy lifestyle and physical fitness and have spoken to many about it. But it wasn't until I decided to sign up for a fitness program and get fit that what I spoke actually carried its weight. Today after having lost close to twenty kilograms I can boldly speak of the benefits of fitness and that people will be inspired to do the same.

CAREER VERSUS CALLING

There's a huge difference between career and calling. Careers are determined by individual ambition while calling is driven by fulfilment and satisfaction. Careers are linked to accomplishment and accolades while calling culminates in a legacy. Career has a temporary time span while the impact of a calling is permanent it is long lasting. There is a retirement age for careers while calling lasts for a lifetime. The outcome for living out your purpose is passion. Passion is contagious. Purpose adds flavour and meaning to the journey of life. Purpose will push you beyond the confines of your comfort zone and help you discover your hidden strengths, potential and abilities which were previously undiscovered. A person of purpose has decided to move ahead of the crowd and not operate with a herd mentality. Purpose will cause you to get off the beaten path and chart your own course. Purpose is more often than not, others-focused and not self-focused. All these guidelines which help you live with purpose when incorporated in leadership can make for a very successful leader.

Although you can participate or contribute to someone else achieving their purpose, you cannot live it out for them. It is essentially internal and intrinsic and individual specific. You cannot outsource the fulfilment of your purpose to someone else. Identifying your purpose is quite easy actually. It is easy if you identify the things that burden you, the things that drive you, the things that you are passionate about and the stuff that keeps you awake at night. These are usually pointers as to what your purpose is. I believe we are born with a purpose. You can choose a career, a vocation, an education but you cannot choose a purpose apart from that which you are wired to accomplish. The rewards of purpose are not measured in terms of economic prosperity. Economic prosperity is incidental when you're pursuing your purpose but the reward is satisfaction. Purpose is measured in terms of contribution and fulfilment. Don't compare or contrast your purpose with that of others. I can't decide to be a musician just because I see a musician who is excelling in his passion. Don't underestimate your purpose which may be one of service in comparison to someone else who may serve his purpose in a more public manner. The pursuit of purpose makes us feel alive as we realise where we fit in the grand scheme of things. It helps us understand what we are meant to do and just why we were created. Our life is good when we are successful but it is made great when we are purposeful!

PURPOSE VERSUS PROPERTY

Each of us is unique. No two of us are alike. Our aspirations, goals, passions, likes and dislikes vary. Why are we so different from each other?

Each of us has a specific purpose.

Success is good and it's something we are taught to go after but after a period of time success will lead to emptiness and eventually it is forgotten. What is long remembered is living a life of purpose. Passion and purpose go hand in hand. Passion is what will wake you up every morning with a renewed sense of purpose. It is what will get you through long hours of work, through the tough seasons of life because you will inherently know that it is all worth something in the end. Passion will eventually help you understand why you were born and what your purpose on earth is.

I know a couple in Hyderabad who live in the outskirts of the city and run a huge dog farm. I visited them since I happen to love dogs and was pleasantly surprised at how beautifully maintained and well managed this multi-acre property was. There were over 100 breeds of dogs and they were sent to every part of the country as required. Some were shipped to the Reserve bank of India some to the airports and various other locations. When I was speaking with the gentleman who owns and runs the farm I was surprised to hear that he was a mechanical engineer by profession who had a passion for dogs and hence started this place. He is now one of the foremost dog breeders in Asia. It also turned out that the land on which the dog farm is located is right at the heart of a Naxalite area. After years of severe Naxalite activity and devastation the people left behind were ravaged, impoverished and abandoned. This man, through his farm, began to rehabilitate the local people by giving them job opportunities, teaching them values and educating their children. Today the entire community has been restored and revived thanks to this one man's passion. Had he not pursued his passion, he might very well have missed out on his life's purpose. What is it you're passionate about?

Purpose always supersedes success. Purpose is not about monetary gain. Success is temporary but living purposefully is what stays on long after us as our legacy. Purpose benefits those around us as they are influenced or positively affected by us living with our purpose in mind. Success on the other hand usually only benefits us personally. Purposeful living impacts many and requires hard work. More importantly I believe it requires a divine connection.

PURPOSE FOR TEAMWORK

At a team level there needs to be synergy towards a common objective. Team members have to be aligned to that objective. The common objective could be the organisation or team's collective purpose and it is imperative that all concerned are aligned towards the purpose. If they are not aligned each would be pulling in different directions which would result in disharmony, chaos and unproductive efforts. If, as an individual, there is a conflict between individual purposes and that of the team it is appropriate that the individual moves on. For example, if you want to be a part of the Missionaries of Charity which is the charitable organisation that Mother Teresa founded, you as an individual would need to have a purpose which is aligned to the organisation's purpose which happens to be helping the downtrodden and suffering, to feed, clothe and bathe them. If this purpose is not something you can identify with, its best you move on since you would end up feeling like a misfit and more importantly you will not be contributing to the organisation in any tangible way. When pursuing purpose as a team it is critical and mandatory that the team leader recruits the team members with great care so that those are selected would own the purpose or vision besides having the desire and required skills to contribute to achieving the goal. Secondly it is vital that the leader clearly articulates to the team what the vision or goal is. Finally, the team leader must ensure that all concerned individuals stay aligned to the team's purpose. As with individual purpose, a team's purpose should always take preference over the individual. If it any point the individual becomes greater than the team, it may result in the team moving off course and losing focus. This is a situation that would need vigilance.

SUCCESS SANS PURPOSE?

You could be successful in the eyes of the society, but that doesn't imply being purposeful. However, when you are purposeful you will also be successful. Success is usually quantified in terms of wealth and popularity while purpose is measured by satisfaction, fulfilment and a positive impact on others' lives. The finest example I have seen of this is the life of Mother Teresa. In many a mind she didn't live a successful life since she didn't have a multimillion enterprise but her life was rife with purpose. This purpose eventually led to a successful life. Successful in the sense of the millions of lives that she rescued, loved, cared for and rehabilitated. Nothing could be more successful than that.

Success is a good thing, don't get me wrong. It's just that success without purpose will end up being about the self and not others.

The greatest tragedy is when people trade the time they are given while alive for pursuing temporal fleeting success which is incidentally relative and miss out on being purposeful. You can choose to live your life for the approval of others or you can decide to follow your life's purpose and find the utmost joy in the pursuit.

Remember- You only grow when you cause others to grow! That's the basic premise of living a life of purpose!

Mental Push-Up for Today:

"The impossible for God is easier than 'child's play'. He specialises in making the impossible possible. Dare to believe God for the impossible."

Do you have an impossible list? Why not? Make one today! List down things you desire to happen that seem impossible or completely out of your control right now. Rub that sceptical look off your face and start writing!

_____

_____

_____

_____

_____

_____

_____

_____

_____

_____

_____

Bookmark this page. Keep praying and trusting God with this list. Revisit it every few weeks. Mark off things that have come to pass and as you do remember to not forget that the God of the Impossible helped you through it.

Mental Push-Up for Today:

"While making a choice, never trade off long term gains for short term benefits."

What are some important choices you have to make in the next few weeks? List them here.

_____

_____

_____

_____

_____

_____

_____

Now, note the benefits of these choices.

Short term benefits   Long-term benefits

_____

_____

_____

_____

_____

_____

_____

Mental Push-Up for Today:

"Choices have consequences...You cannot make the wrong choice and expect the right consequence."

Are you facing the consequences of some wrong choices you've made in the past? If so, what were the better choices you could've made in those situations and how might they have helped you? Writing this down will help you choose wisely in the future.

_____

_____

_____

_____

_____

_____

Do you have other important choices that lie ahead of you? Try writing at least two of them down and weighing the possible consequences of these choices before you make them!

_____

_____

_____

_____

_____

_____

Mental Push-Up for Today:

"The moments that precede the breakthrough are often moments of uncertainty, anxiety and a feeling of no control. Don't give in to fear but recognise the fact that God is at work and the breakthrough is underway."

How does this quote apply to you today? Are there areas that you are waiting for a breakthrough in? If so, make a note of them and believe that God will work in them. Do not give in to anxiety and fear.

_____

_____

_____

_____

_____

_____

_____

_____

_____

_____

_____

_____

_____

Mental Push-Up for Today:

"It only takes a little spark to set off a forest fire. So it is with the pursuit of pleasure that derails and distracts you from your purpose. Untamed pleasures are the gateways to your downfall."

Work your brain's biceps. What do you understand from this thought? Write down a few lines on how you can allow this thought to change your lifestyle.

_____

_____

_____

_____

_____

_____

_____

_____

_____

_____

_____

_____

_____

_____

_____

Mental Push-Up for Today:

"Live out your purpose, don't just live to earn a salary. At the end of the day, qualification and designations won't matter but a life of purpose will."

Time to remind yourself of your life purpose statement. Write it again here and also write down how this thought speaks to you today.

_____

_____

_____

_____

_____

_____

_____

_____

_____

_____

_____

_____

_____

Mental Push-Up for Today:

"Fear living a life devoid of purpose more than you fear death."

What are your biggest fears in life? Make note of them here below.

_____

_____

_____

_____

_____

_____

_____

Does deviating from your purpose in life or not fulfilling your purpose scare you? Why?

_____

_____

_____

_____

_____

_____

_____

Mental Push-Up for Today:

"Often blessings come disguised as problems. Don't be deceived by its appearance, if you choose to be patient and endure the temporary hardship you will inherit the blessing."

How can you apply this thought to a situation that you are going through right now?

_____

_____

_____

_____

_____

_____

_____

_____

_____

_____

_____

_____

_____

_____

_____

_____

Mental Push-Up for Today:

"Our breakthroughs, opportunities and breaks often dwell in those things which we postpone and procrastinate."

What are some things that you have been putting off for tomorrow? Make note of them below in order of priority.

_____

_____

_____

_____

_____

_____

_____

How can you over the next few weeks tick off each item on the list above? Assign specific days when you will get to these things.

_____

_____

_____

_____

_____

_____

_____

Mental Push-Up for Today:

"Purpose attracts opposition, nothing significant was ever achieved easily. The degree of opposition is directly proportional to level of significance."

By now, you are sure of what your purpose is. What are the major oppositions to you fulfilling your purpose? What are the things that stand as roadblocks on your journey towards significance?

_____

_____

_____

_____

_____

Do you feel discouraged when you face these challenges? How can you keep yourself focused on your purpose and getting to it?

_____

_____

_____

_____

_____

_____

Mental Push-Up for Today:

"Don't waste half your life believing you can't. What you believe is what will be."

Do you doubt any of your abilities? If so, what are they and why do you doubt them?

_____

_____

_____

_____

_____

_____

_____

How can you overcome these doubts?

_____

_____

_____

_____

_____

_____

_____

Mental Push-Up for Today:

"If you aren't willing to sacrifice it implies that you aren't willing to succeed. Success always requires the investment of sacrifice."

What are some things that you desperately want to achieve? List at least 3 such things down here.

_____

_____

_____

_____

_____

_____

What are the things you must sacrifice to achieve the above list of things? Note them down and write down how you plan to do that.

_____

_____

_____

_____

_____

_____

Mental Push-Up for Today:

"Being purposeful supersedes being successful."

What is your personal definition of success?

_____

_____

_____

_____

Is it possible to be pursuing both success and purpose at the same time? How?

_____

_____

_____

_____

Are you someone who is purposely pursuing success or successfully pursuing purpose?

_____

_____

_____

_____

Mental Push-Up for Today:

"Failure is not so much an outcome of an event but it is a consequence when one gives up and stops trying."

What are some failures that you have experienced in the past year? Note them below.

_____

_____

_____

_____

How did you feel after the failure? Did it encourage you to try again or give up? Either way, what was your natural response?

_____

_____

_____

_____

How can you review the situations and plan more attempts at the same thing you failed in?

_____

_____

_____

_____

_____

Mental Push-Up for Today:

"How far you go in life is largely dependent on how you respond to the question "How hard are you prepared to work?"

Would you call yourself a "hard worker?" Justify your response with reasons and examples.

_____

_____

_____

_____

What are the areas in which you can start working harder to achieve the goals set before you?

_____

_____

_____

_____

How can you keep yourself motivated to keep working hard despite the circumstances?

_____

_____

_____

_____

_____

WISDOM IN COMMUNICATION

Relationship is the glue that keeps our world together. The difference between good relationships and great relationships is the effort put into retaining those relationships.

My relationship with my God is by far the most critical relationship in my life. I have found personally that if my relationship with my creator is not solid then try as I may, I find it hard to get other aspects of my life in order. I also find that I lack peace when my relationship with God is lagging. We need to choose to live life according to the specifications we were created with so that we can live out the potential we are endowed with and experience a life of purpose. Having an ongoing interactive relationship with my God helps me do just that and more.

Every man-made object has a certain purpose for which it is made. If the object is used without an idea of its purpose it is possible to wreck it and get nothing out of it. Just like a phone or any gadget comes with an operating manual in order for us to use it in the way it is meant to be used, a relationship with the one who made us is essential in order for us to discover the purpose of our life while on earth. I'm created and wired a certain way for a specific purpose.

My relationship with my wife and children is most important to me after my relationship with God. Accolades and accomplishments at work are meaningless unless I am a good husband and father at home. As a man it is important that I rise up as the head of the house. It doesn't mean I act like an authoritarian but that I am a loving and caring husband to my wife and try to meet her needs to the best of my abilities. It also means that I am my children's best friend as well as their guide and coach. Bringing them up in the right way while being there for them in every area of their lives.

Like I mentioned earlier, relationships need nurture and care but most importantly they need communication. I can't expect to have a great relationship with my wife or children if I am going to neglect communicating with them. Every relationship needs wise communication as it is the cornerstone of a good relationship. The Bible says that the tongue has the power of life and death which means that I can either build up or tear down a person just by the way I speak to them. I remember as a boy, my mother would constantly speak words of affirmation and encouragement to me irrespective of how I performed or behaved. I found that the more I heard these words of encouragement, the more I believed it and the more I believed it the more I acted on it. So primarily to communicate wisely we need to speak words that build up the people around us. My wife Judith is a great cook, but I have found that when I take the time to appreciate a dish that she cooks it encourages her and also pushes her to outdo herself in her culinary skills. Also important are words that heal another. Very often in our efforts to get academic excellence out of our children, we can tend to be harsh or tough on them. But it's not too late to speak words of healing to them that can undo months and even years of damage our words could have done to them. Many times the things we say even with the best of intentions can come across as harsh because of the way it's said.

I have found that the best method of wise communication is being slow to speak. Thinking before we speak can save us from many a relationship wreck.

Communication involves getting our message across. Period. There are four ways of communicating, namely:

1. Saying the right thing in the wrong way — makes for lost opportunities
2. Wrong thing in the right way — gets you perceived as a radical
3. Wrong thing in the wrong manner — plain foolishness
4. Right thing in the right way — pure wisdom

What kind of communicator are you? Can you identify with any one of the above types of communication? I encourage you to identify your style of communication and begin to work on it. If you are already in the fourth category, then you're good to go. The art of communication is to convey the message, nothing more and nothing less. Effective communication is therefore all about simplicity. It's about expressing yourself and not impressing others.

Words are not the only medium to communicate though. There is body language, posture and your listening ability that count just as much.

I have found from personal experience that the following methods of communication are highly effectual.

1. Communication through story telling
2. Communication using imagery
3. Communication through debate

Stories are a great way to communicate and many times find common ground with people. When narrating a story, you need to not just connect with a person's ears but with their hearts. I have seen that personal stories from one's own life are highly effective tools as they resonate strongly with others who can relate to it on some level or the other.

Communication with images I find helps to retain the message in the minds of the recipients. Good Communicators leverage images from common day scenes in order to illustrate a thought or idea. It not only helps to retain the thought but also significantly simplifies it.

Communication via debate is not always a preferred route but when one has a secure leader who welcomes a challenge to his mandate or is open to a discussion on the pros and cons of a certain idea it presents a great opportunity. If your intentions and motives are clear with no hidden agenda in them then debates can prove to bring about a whole lot of clarity.

CONFLICT RESOLUTION

An inevitable part of communication is the hard task of conflict resolution. The key to successful conflict resolution is asking the right questions.

Common questions that can be asked are "Why do you feel this way?" Or "What could I have done differently?" Or "What exactly happened?"

Asking questions of the person offended helps in getting the facts straight and clearing motives and intents. Right questions are the key to getting the right answers in order to work through conflict.

Conflict resolution sometimes needs the silent treatment. This is especially hard when we are unfairly treated or unjustly accused. Silence in these situations is truly golden and adds to our composure while giving us time to prepare a well thought out response. Once we decide to respond though, we need to be firm and clearly express our point without beating around the bush.

Another thing to remember while resolving conflict is to focus on the issue and not the person as this builds our credibility. Getting personal only makes us vindictive and makes the issue too personal.

OVER COMMUNICATION - A TOOL TO BE WIELDED WISELY

The process of communication is complete only when the person who receives the communication triggers a corresponding response. Until this is achieved, communication is incomplete and needs additional attempts to ensure the right response is got. Often these additional attempts in communication are termed as over communication. Over communication is often recognised as micro management and most often micromanagement is resisted or is viewed as discomforting. However, there are times, especially with certain individual types whose performance is significantly improved with the use of over communication. The trick is to identify these individuals and to use over -communication specifically with them rather than to do so generically, especially while working in a team scenario. However, over communication to convey messages of love, acceptance, self-belief is a must do. Relationships flourish, bonds are strengthened and self-belief blossoms when the right words are spoken and spoken regularly. There is a direct relationship between positive affirmation and high performance. Similarly, there is a direct relationship between negative affirmation and low performance. Largely, performance or strength of relationships varies based on the quantum of communication.

THE ART OF SPEAKING TO A NON-LISTENER

When speaking to an individual who never listens, the most important thing is to be explicit. Be clear that you need their undivided attention for a certain amount of time and that you will answer any questions with them at the end of the conversation. Be precise, specific and clear with what you are going to communicate all the while being cognisant of the person's limited listening skills. It is very important that you don't beat around the bush and have long winded conversations. It will also help to email them a brief of what was discussed post conversation as this will help in the retention of the message. It is important to stay in control of the conversation and steer it back to the topic of discussion when there are diversions or distractions. The choice of place to conduct the discussion also is very important. Choose a place where the person will not be constantly distracted and which will be conducive for a good conversation. Request for mobile phones to be switched off during the course of the conversation and as an example switch off yours first.

Remember, persistence will yield results. Keep at the attempts to communicate and at some point the person will listen just as a response to your perseverance.

AUTHENTIC COMMUNICATION

It is better not to communicate than to be fake while communicating. Communicating well is about expressing and not about impressing. When you are fake in your communication, it will be seen through at some stage and will result in a loss of personal credibility. Someone once said, a single lie can negate a hundred truths that have been spoken. More often than not, you will earn respect for being honest and straight forward in your communication. It is however important that it is communicated in a manner that doesn't dilute the message but is respectful and courteous. It is important to be firm yet respectful. Take a balanced view. Don't sugar coat a message that needs to be articulated in a firm manner. Pay close importance to the tone of your message as well. Often an opportunity to communicate is lost not because the content is incorrect but because the tone was inappropriate. Most importantly choose to be consistent in the way you communicate.

THE POWER OF "YES"

I've seen many people across my career miss out on significant opportunities and stagnate only to regret later because they were closed to taking on new responsibilities, opportunities because they perceived it as a burden, extra work or the fear of doing something new. In the context of any team, you get noticed and stand out not just because of the talent you possess but more importantly as someone who is willing to stretch to do the extra which others don't want to or because you choose to take initiative. Personally I have benefitted by saying yes to certain assignments which have required of me to move cities. In the course of my career of over two decades I have lived out of seven cities and have had to move lock, stock and barrel. This forced me to hunt for school admission, houses and adapt to new cultures. It was tough and even intimidating I must confess but in hindsight I'm glad I said yes because these moves and these opportunities have served to fast track my career. It's important to say yes and seize the opportunity but there are a few guidelines to follow before saying yes.

- Say yes to things that align with your value system
- Say yes to things that align with your priorities
- Say yes if that opens up opportunities to learn new things
- Say yes only if you want to and not merely because others want you to
- Say yes when you are in a position or you have a clear plan to complete the task at hand and to complete it well
- Don't let fear prevent you from saying Yes

Most importantly, you won't always have the whole view but as long as you understand the vision and can see the immediate steps say yes. Then eventually you will see the rest of the steps that you will need to take and ultimately the picture will reach its completion.

THE POWER OF "NO"

Saying No is the single most powerful tool in great communication in order to live a life of character, integrity and purpose. Many times we cave in to pressure to behave in a certain way or do a certain thing just to get the approval of friends and co-workers. But the Bible tells us that our "Yes" should be Yes and our "No" be no. The syndrome of peer pressure can debilitate us and keep us crippled from embracing the change that we may really need in our life. Wisdom is knowing when to say No and when to not say No. It's the difference between reaching our full potential or making a wrong choice which can cost us a lot.

In my life, saying no saved me from getting back into destructive addictions.

I have had to say no to certain groups of people and certain situations which would have tempted me to go back down into an abyss of old habits. The short term pain of saying no is better for the joy of long term pleasure.

Mental Push-Up for Today:

"To change outcomes, change your response to events that you face. Events that you experience are not controllable but your responses are."

Here's some cardio for your mind: Make a note of at least three situations that you are dealing with currently which are out of your control.

_____

_____

_____

_____

How can you change your response to these situations?

_____

_____

_____

_____

Recall a situation this week when you responded well to a situation. You should be proud of yourself and write it down so that you don't forget it easily!

_____

_____

_____

_____

_____

Mental Push-Up for Today:

"Resist the urge to answer in a rush. Take a minute, think, process and then respond. Many a conflict will be avoided and this approach will result in a favourable outcome."

Proverbs 15:28 – "The mind of the uncompromisingly righteous studies how to answer, but the mouth of the wicked pours out evil things."

Think of situations when you have spoken too soon or responded without thought. Jot them down. It might be difficult or embarrassing to do so but nonetheless make detailed note of at least three such situations.

_____

_____

_____

_____

_____

Here's some cardio for thought: What would you have rather said in those situations?

_____

_____

_____

_____

_____

_____

Mental Push-Up for Today:

"Five Principles of an effective communicator: Don't just think but meditate, don't just read but study, don't just hear but listen, don't just talk but communicate and don't just reach out to others but connect with them."

According to this quote, what are the most important things to keep in mind about being a more effective communicator?

_____

_____

_____

_____

_____

_____

Communication Challenge: Which of these things do you feel you need to start doing more? Make a note of them here and write down how you plan to go about them.

_____

_____

_____

_____

_____

_____

Mental Push-Up for Today:

"The manifestation of wisdom is the ability to control one's anger and the manifestation of maturity is to overlook an offence."

Proverbs 19:11 – "Good sense makes one slow to anger, and it is his glory to overlook an offence…"

Are you the Incredible Hulk? Do you react in anger when provoked in certain situations? What are the things or situations that make you react like this? It is important that you note them down.

_____

_____

_____

_____

_____

_____

How can you work towards controlling your anger in such situations?

_____

_____

_____

_____

_____

_____

Mental Push-Up for Today:

"Often the best response during a conflict is no response."

Proverbs 26:4-5 – "Do not answer a fool according to his folly, or you yourself will be just like him. Answer a fool according to his folly, or he will be wise in his own eyes."

It's time to stretch your mental muscles again. Write down what your usual reaction is when you are in the centre of a conflict.

_____

_____

_____

_____

_____

_____

_____

How can you use today's *Wisdom Workout* to change the way you react in conflict?

_____

_____

_____

_____

_____

_____

_____

Mental Push-Up for Today:

"The fact is that our lives speak louder than our mouth. People are influenced, inspired and impacted by the quality of our lives rather than the eloquence of our speech."

Apply this quote to your day today. Cascade it down into ONE action point. What can you do today that will reflect this thought?

_____

_____

_____

_____

_____

_____

_____

_____

_____

_____

_____

_____

_____

_____

Mental Push-Up for Today:

"When angry, force yourself to speak softly."

Proverbs 15:1 – "A soft answer turns away wrath, but a harsh word stirs up wrath."

Anger Management Buddy:

Here's an interesting project you can take on for a week if you want to really work on responding better when you are angry.

When provoked to react in anger, before you say a single word, pull out your smartphone or a notepad and write down what you want to say to the person you are upset with. REFRAIN from saying it to them. Just write it down. Now, read back to yourself what you have written down and consider rephrasing it with kind words and a soft tone and then speak it to the person. Make a note here of how this worked or didn't work in your favour throughout the week.

_____

_____

_____

_____

_____

_____

_____

_____

Mental Push-Up for Today:

"You talk to *you* more than others talk to *you;* so take care to speak wisely."

Use adjectives to describe the kind of words that you speak to yourself.

_____

_____

_____

_____

Are these the kind of words that build you up? If not, what can you do to change them drastically so that they become edifying?

_____

_____

_____

_____

Note some practical steps you will take towards speaking positively to yourself or thinking positive thoughts about yourself?

_____

_____

_____

_____

_____

Mental Push-Up for Today:

"*No* is a good word, use it well. Don't end up saying *Yes* to everything."

Do you have trouble saying *No*? If your answer is *No*, clearly you don't have to worry! If *Yes*, write down what makes you feel compelled to say *Yes* to every situation or person or work you come across.

_____

_____

_____

_____

_____

_____

What do you fear will happen if you say *No*?

_____

_____

_____

_____

_____

_____

_____

Mental Push-Up for Today:

"Wisdom is knowing when to speak up and when to shut up!"

Do you consider yourself to be someone who speaks up at the right time? Note instances when you wish you had spoken up and expressed your opinion.

_____

_____

_____

_____

Do you also have memories of instances when you wish you hadn't spoken something? Make a note of them below.

_____

_____

_____

_____

Can you find someone to be accountable to where your speech is considered?

_____

_____

_____

_____

_____

_____

Mental Push-Up for Today:

"Resist the urge to answer in a rush, take a minute to think, process and then respond. Many a conflict will be avoided and this approach will result in a favourable outcome!"

Can you think of situations in which you have reacted in haste without taking time to think? Note them below.

_____

_____

_____

_____

Now that you have time to think, how would you have rather responded in those situations?

_____

_____

_____

_____

Can you think of one conflict that was avoided by you thanks to some thought before you spoke? Write it down below.

_____

_____

_____

_____

_____

Mental Push-Up for Today:

"A gossip betrays a confidence, but a trustworthy person keeps a secret." - Proverbs 11:13

Are you someone who can keep a secret well? Do your friends trust you? If yes, what is it about you that make them trust you so much?

_____

_____

_____

_____

Have you been in situations where you've either broken someone's trust or where someone has broken your trust? How did that make you feel?

_____

_____

_____

_____

What can you actively do to become someone more trustworthy?

_____

_____

_____

_____

_____

Mental Push-Up for Today:

"Don't "jump to a conclusion" rather "pursue facts" when arriving at a decision."

How does this thought apply to any situation you are facing currently? Note down your thoughts.

_____

_____

_____

_____

_____

_____

_____

_____

_____

_____

_____

_____

_____

_____

WISDOM IN RELATIONSHIPS

We spend a significant portion of our twenty-four hours at the workplace and hence it is imperative to go to a happy place daily. Having worked for a little more than two decades, I am convinced that people contribute, respond, participate and are more committed when there is an established healthy, caring relationship in place. When I look back at my career, what gives me the greatest satisfaction apart from the awards and the accolades is the fact that former team members continue to stay in touch and there is a genuine warmth and affection that continues to remain despite not being team members currently or the fact that time has lapsed. I once had the very difficult task of asking one of my team members to resign given the prevalent situation within the organisation. I had to take the decision but because of the strength of our relationship he accepted it well and continues to stay in touch, be a good friend and asks for my advice and guidance. As it turns out, today, he is a successful entrepreneur. Develop and nurture relationships that are beyond mere transactions in nature. The oft repeated quote that people don't leave organisations but leave bosses is so true. Treat people as people not as machinery or objects. Inspire their minds and appeal to their emotions. Great relationships at work happen when you appreciate the worth of each individual. Collaboration at the work place will result in greater engagement resulting in greater productivity compared to competition which will on the other hand, result in the creation of silos and disengagement in teams at large.

BOSS-SUBORDINATE RELATIONSHIP

A good leader is one who is available and approachable. By available I mean that he has time for his team members. Some leaders are so absorbed in their individual work or are too busy to make time for their team, especially when their team members need them the most. This will create a vacuum in the relationship. What I mean by approachable is that they are prepared and open for what team members have to say. If they aren't approachable, it will result in walls being built up and a breakdown in communication. They sometimes end up listening to what they prefer to hear rather than what they need to hear. They would rather gloss over uncomfortable topics rather than meet it head on. This is not good for the relationship. It's great therefore to share a relationship of professional comfort.

PROFESSIONAL COMFORT

I carefully chose the word professional because there's a thin line of protocol that needs to be adhered to, in the absence of which work ethic could potentially be threatened and in some cases give rise to direct or passive insubordination. I realised that having lunch with the team is a great way to develop and strengthen professional comfort amongst team members. It's in instances like these where you end up discussing non- work related stuff which increases the comfort level and breaks down inhibitions between team members.

So what is professional comfort? It's when you as a team member have provided access and space for a team member to share his or her mind without inhibitions. When you show care and empathy you are actually practicing professional comfort. When you build confidence and strengthen relationships by involving the team in group activities such as watching a movie together or playing a sport together, professional comfort is further established. Celebrating individual success as if it's your own success is also a great way to build professional comfort. Not showing favouritism or partiality but being just and fair is another great way to nurture this culture. It's important that while one increases professional comfort that they don't get too close for comfort. Avoid getting personal but continue to remain professional in order to retain professional comfort at the work spot.

FOSTERING GOOD RELATIONSHIPS BETWEEN TEAM MEMBERS

Diversity between members of a team is a given and it is a strength. However, a team remains united through a common goal, a common objective and by an effective leader. Tampering with the diversity of a team will be counter- productive and could eliminate intrinsic strengths. The methods that a leader could employ to cultivate good relationships in his team could involve leading by collaboration instead of competition. I'm not against competition but I'm definitely pro collaboration. Collaboration not only yields positive results on a short term basis but on a sustainable basis in the long run. A weak leader would spur a particular team member to compete with another with an intent to increase productivity. This could possibly yield the desired results in the short term but it could be the start of rivalry and a souring of the relationship. On the other hand, collaboration gives the opportunity for the team to synergise, strategize, problem solve and more importantly, achieve together. This provides the ideal soil for great relationships. It's important that the leader sets and states clear expectations. For instance, make gossip a strict no-no within the team. Articulate clearly the rules regarding conflict management. Team activities help to increase bonding between team members so make it a part of the regular agenda. Transparency is a must in creating healthy team dynamics. Leading by example is a prerequisite for a leader to create a healthy culture in his team. After all, when all is said and done, it's not all that the leader says that impacts his team but more of what he actually does. Finally, be firm with offenders who directly or indirectly break the rules of engagement or endanger harmony of the team.

PERSONAL RELATIONSHIPS AND WORK

Balance is key to effective, purposeful and successful living. I do believe that a healthy personal relationship will directly contribute to performance at work and business. Strong relationships at the domestic front will also act as a cushion to absorb pressure at work. Discussing work related issues with the family helps in allowing one to de-stress and also others to contribute via ideas and encouragement. As far as possible avoid bringing work home. An individual plays multiple roles. Roles like a father, husband, son, mother, daughter and wife besides being a boss, subordinate, employer of employee. Every role is equally important. Hence when one moves into a particular role it is important that one plays that important role to the best of their ability. In my life, at home I play the role of a husband and a father. If I consistently don't play that role when and where I'm supposed to, then I fail. Hence balance is vital and key. Similarly, during work hours, I need to play the role of an employee or a functional role. I cannot allow my personal life to distract me from this role during the time that I spend at work. Balance is key to a person of purpose.

MISUNDERSTANDINGS IN RELATIONSHIPS

Any relationship will have its share of misunderstandings. So expecting otherwise is to live in fool's paradise. What is crucial is to deal with these misunderstandings and not ignore them as they will prove to be cancerous in the long run. Few practical steps to resolve misunderstanding are

- **Eliminate ego.**

Ego is a false sense of pride. Ego does more damage than bullets and weapons. Many a relationship has been broken by a powerful ego.

- **Fight the issue and not the person.**

Many times during a conflict it becomes a war of personalities. Don't fight the person. Instead identify the issue and separate it from the person. I have found in conflict resolution when the distinction is made between the personality and the issue much progress can be made to rectify the relationship as there is lesser animosity between the individuals.

- **Agree to disagree respectfully.**

We will not and need not agree to everything that is discussed with the other person but choose to disagree respectfully. Don't be afraid to admit you made a mistake. This will strengthen your relationship. Don't let pride get in the way. The converse is also true. If you are in the position of offering forgiveness, go for it. It will work for the betterment of the relationship. Offering forgiveness and apologising are not signs of weakness but of immense strength. Find common grounds to agree on especially when you are taking extreme positions. It's a great way to resolve the conflict.

- **Avoid speaking behind another's back.**

This is a good rule of thumb to follow. Not just during times of conflict but in general, avoid speaking behind a person s back. Human nature will make us want to discuss with others how unfairly we have been treated, what was told to us, who was responsible for our present situation etc. but it really should be avoided at all costs. The reason being that the emotional response to a conflict causes us to say many things that we may later regret and which could cause a greater misunderstanding. So instead a direct approach response is almost always preferred. Speaking directly to the concerned person at the right time in the right way will show that you are mature. Remember that you are not always right. For that matter no one is always right. So reconsider and re-evaluate your stand.

- **Put the organisational and team's goal ahead of personal issues.**

Make sure that throughout the conflict and its resolution that the team and organisation's goals and productivity are not being hampered. If that happens it will directly reflect on you and cause bigger issues to deal with.

- **Reconciliation means forgetting.**

This forgetting is not a momentary lapse in memory but a permanent deletion of the conflict from your mind. The reason I emphasize this is because a partial forgetting will cause the conflict to get rehashed in the most inconvenient of times. This will not work to the benefit of the team or the individuals concerned. So be prepared to forgive and really FORGET!

GOOD RELATIONSHIPS VERSUS SUCCESS AT THE WORK PLACE

Good relationships are one of the valuable lessons that life has to offer. So it would be unwise to sacrifice relationships for any reason. But we do need to be wise about the relationships we choose to be in since any relationship allows a certain degree of access. This access makes you open to the influence that the other person could expose you to either directly or indirectly. Influence that is positive is very beneficial however negative influences can be a distraction. Not everyone is going to like you. That's a fact of life. It's important to admit it, accept it and deal with it. Don't waste your precious time trying to please everyone. The people pleasing rut will cause you to lose your originality, your individuality and will leave you feeling disillusioned and disappointed. Frankly, it's none of our business what others think of us. As long you act in an ethical and honest manner, while being true to your conscience and to who you are, you have nothing to worry about. I'm a believer in the fact that the quality of work you do, the accountability that you display and stewardship are key ingredients to get you ahead. It might take longer than you expect but it will surely promote you. Politicking at the workplace is an unfortunate reality. The degree of politicking might vary from one organisation to another but the effects are always detrimental to the working of the organisation. Those who indulge in it intend to get ahead by pulling others down and usually operate out of a place of insecurity. In the long run these people will be exposed for what they really are about. Excellence is a magnet and will attract elevation.

On the contrary petty politics and stepping on others will have no reward.

THE "BOSS" FACTOR

The popular quote which says you can't choose your parents or your boss is really true. Every individual has a unique temperament like I mentioned earlier and it is critical that the uniqueness is recognised and respected. A leader is respected when he or she stands up for his/her team. An integral quality of leadership is to be generous and not selfish. When personal ambition of a leader is a driving factor often the interests of the team members take a back seat. This spells clear disaster for a team. As a leader it is important to balance the welfare and interests of the team as well as align the expectations of his or her supervisor with the team. As a manager of a team it is imperative that one can withstand the pressure and stress exerted by the supervisor and not transfer it to the team members. Wisdom is required to communicate the same to get productive action and desired results. Avoid either bad mouthing your fellow teammates to your boss or vice versa. Both adversely affect relationships.

Invest more time in mentoring, guiding, training and monitoring progress among your team members than trying to impress your boss.

The overarching principle I follow is to "Do unto others as you would have them do to you." Which means you would need to be the kind of boss to your team members that you want your boss to be to you.

ACCOUNTABILITY IN RELATIONSHIPS

Accountability is a key requisite anywhere, especially at the work place. The sooner we take responsibility and choose to be accountable, the faster we will make progress. We are all dealt a deck of cards. In them we will find great cards, not so great cards and some plain old bad cards. Instead of cribbing and complaining about the not-so-good cards and worse, still comparing our cards with those of others, choose to make the best use of the cards you have been dealt. Accountability is an individual and internal trait. It is about taking ownership no matter what cards we have been dealt with. If we stop worrying about who gets the credit and work on achieving the goal, we would make far more progress. A good leader passes on the credit when things go well and takes responsibility when things don't go as planned. You demonstrate accountability when you choose not to pass the buck but decide to persevere with the task or project till it is done no matter what obstacles you may face. Accountability doesn't look for why things don't work rather it works on the principle of why not. Accountability is not so focused on the reward but rather on the satisfaction of completing a task. Accountability is all about finishing well rather than starting with a bang. Accountability doesn't mean saying yes to every task but means that we carefully choose what can be completed well realistically. Accountability on a personal level isn't about the applause and appreciation but about the fulfilment and inner satisfaction that it gives you on the long run. Accountability opens doors for higher responsibility.

Mental Push-Up for Today:

"You could embrace ego and destroy relationships or eliminate ego and build relationships. Choose well!"

Work your thought muscles. Write down what you think is the root of ego.

_____

_____

_____

_____

_____

Think about this: Is there a relationship in your life that is being destroyed because of ego? Write about it here if you want to.

_____

_____

_____

_____

What can you practically do to build this relationship?

_____

_____

_____

_____

_____

Mental Push-Up for Today:

"Don't find excuses, find time. Time is the fuel through which relationships are built."

List here below the most important relationships in your life right now.

_____

_____

_____

_____

How much time in a week do you invest in each of these relationships? If you aren't investing time in some of them, have those relationships suffered consequently?

_____

_____

_____

_____

_____

How can you move things around in your weekly schedule to make more time for people that matter in your life?

_____

_____

_____

_____

_____

Mental Push-Up for Today:

"It really doesn't matter what levels of success you achieve, if your relationships at home are broken."

Honesty Zone: Are you someone who prioritizes work or other interests over family? If so, why?

_____

_____

_____

_____

Write about a relationship at home that isn't quite what you want it to be. Is it broken? Is it just a bit uncomfortable? Or has it been ignored on your part?

_____

_____

_____

_____

_____

Write down steps you want to take in the next few days to work on this relationship you mentioned above.

_____

_____

_____

_____

_____

Mental Push-Up for Today:

"Relationships are more about giving than receiving; it's ironical though, the more you give, the more you end up receiving."

Do people you are closely associated with consider you a 'giver'? Write here below, your response and why you think it is true.

_____

_____

_____

_____

It's time to assess! Are there certain relationships in your life that you feel the need to 'give' more time, effort and resources into? How do you plan to do that?

_____

_____

_____

_____

Do you know someone who is always giving and blesses you a lot through their selfless generosity? Write about them. What can you learn from them?

_____

_____

_____

_____

Mental Push-Up for Today:

"There is a direct co-relation between the ability to forgive and the durability of a relationship."

Are you generally a forgiving person? If not, why not? What are your struggles with forgiveness?

_____

_____

_____

_____

_____

_____

Is there someone in your life now who you need to forgive? Can you let go of any grudge you have against this person? Write down how you plan to reconcile with them?

_____

_____

_____

_____

_____

_____

Mental Push-Up for Today:

"Most people are misunderstood before they are understood. Take time to understand."

Most relationships are strained because of misunderstanding. Do you have any relationships in your life now that have any issues in them? Write about the issue and consider how it might be a misunderstanding? How you plan to resolve this issue?

_____

_____

_____

_____

_____

_____

Are you misunderstood a lot? Why is it? How can you make people understand you better?

_____

_____

_____

_____

_____

_____

Mental Push-Up for Today:

"A good relationship isn't a game of dumb charades; it is important to explicitly express your feelings, emotions and affection."

Do you struggle to express yourself in any relationship? Why?

_____

_____

_____

_____

How can you work on better expressing yourself in some important relationships in your life? What are some steps you will take?

_____

_____

_____

_____

Is there someone in your life who constantly expresses to you their feelings and emotions? How does this help your relationship? How can you reciprocate?

_____

_____

_____

_____

_____

Mental Push-Up for Today:

"Money is often recognised as the evidence of being blessed, this isn't true. The accurate proof of being blessed is the ability to be a blessing to others."

Think about your life goals. Do they revolve around gaining wealth or being a blessing to others? Write them down here and see how you can make them more 'others' focused.

_____

_____

_____

_____

_____

_____

Think about people you can be a blessing to, anyone in need whom you can reach out to in your circle of influence. Write their names down and make an effort through this month to be a blessing to them!

_____

_____

_____

_____

_____

_____

_____

WISDOM IN LEADERSHIP

I believe that leadership is the ability to influence. It is often mistaken as a designation or a title. If you are in a position of influence, you have the potential to practice leadership. While some individuals have the opportunities to lead teams, there are those who don't have that responsibility but are meant to support, encourage and assist the said leaders. In no way are they inferior to those who have the task of leadership. When you study the life history of many famous leaders you will find that they had an inner circle. A group of people who encouraged, supported and sometimes even corrected them. These people were not celebrities, in fact, very little is known about them, yet their contribution to their leader was invaluable.

I also believe that if you cannot consistently work at leading yourself, you are not in a position to lead others. We all consciously or unconsciously want to manage others but management begins with managing oneself. In today's world of instant communication and social media, you could easily and efficiently influence others through leadership blogs, thoughts, books and posts.

One goes through periods of preparation for leadership. During these phases, it is critical that you observe and learn the lessons that you need to learn. It might feel like you are stagnating without any real progress, but the key to this period is to not give up. Though it will be tempting to get distracted or even quit during these times, if you do give in and call it a day you could very well abort some excellent leadership opportunities.

WAITING TO BE A LEADER? THIS IS FOR YOU!

Wait. Your time will come. There is no point in being impatient and impulsive because you will end up doing things that you will regret.

While you are waiting, learn. It is important that your waiting period is used efficiently and effectively. There is purpose in your waiting. Most often the purpose is to learn the lessons that you need to learn while waiting by observing, reading and relating. Pick up these valuable lessons on leadership so that when you are formally given the position to lead others you can put all these lessons into practice.

Gather leadership lessons by choosing to be mentored. There is no better learning method than by being mentored by someone who has already walked the path that you currently tread on. They will not just speak out of theory but actual life experience. This transfer of wisdom will stand you in good stead when you are in a position of leadership.

Good leadership thrives on discipline. Develop and work on pursuing a lifestyle of discipline.

Leadership is developed or derailed by the choices you make. Be careful of the choices you make while you wait.

There should be a synergy between your talk and your walk. This means you have got to practice what you preach.

Lead from where you are. Lead well those who are in your circle of influence in either a formal or informal way so that when leadership is formally handed to you, you will be fully prepared.

Leadership needs a great attitude. During your period of waiting let go of all negative attitudes and emotions so that you are well prepared for the period of leadership.

You will be handed formal leadership opportunities when you display personal excellence. Make sure that in your work that quality is uncompromised.

A good leader needs great interpersonal skills which means you have to cultivate and maintain good relationships even before you become a leader so that these relationships only grow after you are made a leader.

TIPS TO BEING A GREAT FOLLOWER

Remember that unless you are a good follower you cannot be a good leader. That is a time tested fact. It is critical that you follow the right person. Who you choose to follow will determine your destiny.

A prerequisite to following is to carry out instruction. Another meaning of following is obeying. If you are unable to follow instructions given it would be hard to be a follower.

Following involves first unlearning before learning. We all have a lot of life experiences which can deter us from moving forward in our pursuit of leadership. They can cause beliefs that could be detrimental to our progress. I call this the principle of the sponge. You know that a sponge can absorb water or any other liquid as long as it's empty or wrung dry. It's the same with our mind unlearning in order to learn.

Another important principle for a follower is being unafraid to ask questions. It's important to clarify and sometimes even to disagree but disagreement handled the wrong way can lead to rebellion. Rebellion is a big no-no. Rebellion will start manifesting in actions and attitudes which therefore have to be kept in check.

It is important to be vulnerable in order to be a great follower. Be yourself to those who you choose to be led by. If you decide to pretend to be someone else, it will not benefit you even if you are led by the right people. It is important that your leader is aware of your strengths and more importantly your weaknesses. That *knowledge* is very important for the leader to effectively guide and train you.

Correction is very important for the learning process. Don't resist it or be put off by it. While appreciation is good, correction for the right reasons will benefit immensely and reap rich rewards.

Humility and being submissive to the leader are pre requisites of a follower. Pride has got no place. Submission is a trait of great leadership and is birthed from being a great follower. There will come times when you will have different ideas or different ways of thinking but if there ever comes a time when the follower thinks he is superior to the leader it could spell disaster for the follower since there could be a loss of valuable wisdom transfer from the leader to him. Stay humble as that's the vital ingredient to excellent leadership.

Mental Push-Up for Today:

"Leadership is a 24/7 assignment, there are no timeouts. Leadership is not just about delivering an inspirational speech rather it is about leading by example. The essence of leadership is to promote others and not self. Leadership and vision are inseparable."

What areas are you a leader in? Note them down below.

_____

_____

_____

_____

What are the leadership lessons from this quote that you can apply immediately and how?

_____

_____

_____

_____

As a leader in your area of influence, do you have a vision? As a part of your *Wisdom Workout* today, write down your vision statement here.

_____

_____

_____

_____

Mental Push-Up for Today:

"Great leaders focus more on people than results. They are conscious of the fact that when they take care of people, results take care of themselves."

How can you apply this thought to your leadership role at work and at your circles of influence?

_____

_____

_____

_____

_____

_____

Be a _Wisdom Workout_ coach yourself! Today, make note of two people in your team that you want to focus on, mentor and take care of. This could be someone you've probably overlooked in the past or not paid much attention to.

_____

_____

_____

_____

_____

_____

Mental Push-Up for Today:

"The reason we are endowed with gifts and talents is not so that we exhibit superiority, or flaunt our ability neither is it to advertise ourselves before others. The sole purpose of gifts and talents is to serve one another as faithful stewards."

Honesty Zone: What are the gifts you have that you take great pride in? How can you apply this thought to how you use your gifts to serve others?

_____

_____

_____

_____

_____

_____

_____

_____

_____

_____

_____

_____

_____

_____

_____

Mental Push-Up for Today:

"Leadership is about giving credit to those it is due to when things go well and taking responsibility when things go wrong. It is never the other way around."

Who is someone in your team or someone you work with that needs to be given credit for what they do? Write down their names and what they contribute and how you can appreciate them.

_____

_____

_____

_____

_____

Has something in your direct line of responsibility gone wrong lately? Write it down and note steps to how you place to take responsibility and make up for it.

_____

_____

_____

_____

_____

_____

Mental Push-Up for Today:

"A sign of a good leader is the willingness to apologise. Honour such leaders."

Think about mistakes you've made with the people or team that you are leading. Have you apologised for those mistakes to your team? If so, write down examples of when you have.

_____

_____

_____

_____

If there have been instances when you found it difficult to apologise, what are the things that stopped you from doing so? What were your biggest fears?

_____

_____

_____

_____

What steps can you take to overcome these fears and become a leader that isn't afraid to say sorry?

_____

_____

_____

_____

_____

Mental Push-Up for Today:

"A trait of a good leader is the ability to make every team member believe that what they do individually is critically important for the success of the team."

Write down the names of the people in your team and what their most important strengths are.

_____

_____

_____

_____

_____

_____

_____

Have there been instances where you have struggled to delegate responsibilities according to people's strengths? If so, why? What can you do differently next time you are in a similar situation?

_____

_____

_____

_____

_____

_____

_____

Mental Push-Up for Today:

"People will forget our achievements but will remember our assistance. The tragedy is that we get our priorities mixed up."

In the pursuit of our goals on vision, we often tend to forget about helping those in need around us. So take some time today to think about people around you. Write names of people who are in need and what you can do within your ability to help them in that area of need. Tick off the list as you get through it.

_____

_____

_____

_____

_____

_____

_____

_____

_____

_____

_____

_____

_____

WISDOM IN EXCELLENCE

Mediocrity is a choice. So is excellence. We don't just end up being mediocre or excellent by default. It has to be the result of a conscious decision made, backed by a right action. Excellence is an acquired attribute and a pursuit. It is obtained by deliberate actions. When wisdom is applied to *knowledge* and action, excellence is birthed. When you decide to be excellent you gather *knowledge* through learning and observation besides your personal experiences. You will engage with mentors, develop the right set of habits, learn from failures, choose to constantly and consistently improve and compete with yourself in order to achieve excellence. Excellence will elude you if you're

- comfortable with settling for less
- when compromise is convenient and
- when you play to the applause of people rather than being driven by personal satisfaction.

Rewards and recognition are good but excellence should be the purpose and the goal. It will cause you to be different from everyone else. When I began my career I made one decision. I realised early on that staying with the crowd would not benefit me in any way. Being with the crowd implies that you do only as much as the crowd does. You don't do more than that and try not to do less than that since you're trying to be part of the pack. And in a sense being part of the pack creates a herd mentality which gives you a false sense of security. I say false as I'm not sure how certain this security is since it wouldn't benefit me in any conceivable way.

Excellence required me to be in a position of constant learning. As a result of this I developed the habit of reading every day. Believe me when I say this. It is easier said than done since with long, hard days at work it's almost impossible to muster the strength to sit with a book. I made it a habit therefore to read a minimum of ten pages a day which in reality is not that big of a burden. I keep myself updated of advances in my area of expertise and apart from that I read anything that stimulates me positively. In hindsight this habit has helped me to use my mental faculties well and in many ways impacted my subconscious mind.

I then chose to be an idea hunter, always on the lookout for ideas. Ideas are everywhere we just need to keep an eye out for new ideas. The best example is learning about new generation businesses which are raking in tremendous profits, touching lives, impacting people and breaking geographic boundaries in their reach. Take Facebook for example. Nothing better than an application that connects people across countries and that helps people stay in touch irrespective of geographical constraints. Consider UBER. What a great idea to have the issue of conveyance made easy just with the click of a button on our phones. There are medical aggregators today through which you can find doctors and book appointments at leisure and so also hotel aggregators which make holidaying all too easy. There are so many other great ideas out there today. Today's businesses are run more on ideas and innovation than on machinery.

TODAY'S RAW MATERIALS ARE IDEAS...

I usually keep my Saturdays to generate ideas. I listen to TED talks, read up on Harvard business reviews and try to dig up ideas. I look for problems and challenges that businesses face and look for solutions.

I also have a monthly 'hour of power' I choose to call it, with my mentor. I share my goals, my successes, my failures and struggles with him and really feed on the ensuing conversation. It's these meetings that really shape me and give me a renewed perspective on many things. It is very important to choose a mentor carefully. Be wise as to who you allow access to influence your life. The power of influence will either drive you to success or plummet you to mediocrity. So who are you opening up to in order to influence you? Do you have someone who can effectively mentor and shape you? Personally, I am very careful as to who mentors me. And that one hour a month is of high priority to me.

PERSEVERANCE IS THE FUEL FOR EXCELLENCE

The level of excellence you achieve will be directly related to the level of perseverance. There have been times when I've hit rock bottom with the various roadblocks and challenges I have faced and honestly was ready to throw in the towel. But during those times I worked hard to focus on the end state of the goal. What is the fulfilment of this goal? What benefit will this have for the organisation? How does this help my community and how does it benefit me as an individual? What's the experience that I've gained? So when these thoughts are on my mind, hitting a road block only serves to revitalize me and refocus my attention on what is critical at that point.

BE PREPARED

The final thing that enhances a spirit of excellence is anticipating obstacles and preparing for them in advance. That way when I encounter an obstacle I don't go into a slump but instead have a plan that I can begin to execute.

EXCELLENCE COMES AT A PRICE

How you use your time is foundational. Who you hang out with, what's the trade off your willing to make, what risks are you willing to take, how much of criticism are you willing to absorb? These are questions that you should be prepared to answer in order to achieve excellence.

I was confronted with this in my life recently after a routine visit to the doctor. After the usual height, weight and related parameters being checked the doctor told me that my body age (first time I even heard this word) was twelve years ahead of my chronological age. This report shocked me and urged me to take stock of my health and fitness. I then decided to visit a dietician and subsequently made quite a few changes in my diet. For the next ten weeks I consciously avoided choice food (not the easiest course of action with the holiday season coming on) and began waking up at five in the morning to work out at the gym. Up until then, I had been an on again off again visitor to the gym but now I began to walk five kms on the treadmill on a daily basis. The result? In ten weeks I lost 18 kgs. I started out at 97.6 kgs and dropped down to 79.5 kgs. It was tough but it was satisfying. I was now healthier, stronger and well within my required BMI range. And when I say healthier I really mean it for I was a frequent user of the Asthalin inhaler up until then. By frequent, I mean dependent. The allowed usage of the inhaler is for a maximum of three times a day, but I used to use it around twenty-two times a day, needing it even to ascend a small flight of stairs. Now, thanks to the fitter version of me, I don't need the inhaler at all. Worth the effort? I think so. The same principles I used for my fitness can be applied in any area of your life that needs a boost of excellence. It will come at a price but worth every penny!

WORKING HARD VERSUS WORKING SMART

Which one wins you ask? Well, both are equally important. I know that sounds anti-climactic but it's true. Working hard involves putting in the hard yards, pursuing the process and discipline to stick to a regime. The fact is that your results are never greater than your efforts. Wishing will not get your results but working will. Working hard is indispensable. You have to be willing to work hard to get the results you want. Working smart involves doing things in the right time in the right way. Working smart is not about taking short cuts but definitely about doing what is important and doing those tasks which yield maximum benefits rather than those which yield minimum or no benefits. Working smart involves constantly looking for ways to improve the process required. It requires you to be flexible, nimble and agile. My belief is that there are situations where you are required to work hard while there are other specific situations where you could work smart.

An example of a worker on a factory floor is of someone who needs to work hard in following standard operating procedure. Experimenting with the standard operating procedure or being careless is not an option as it could lead to serious and disastrous consequences. On the other hand, innovations and breakthroughs require a consistent mindset to challenge the paradigm, the current process to explore opportunities from problems and obstacles. The synergy of working hard and working smart are highly essential for excellence to be achieved. Apple is an example of an organisation who consistently works on innovation and this is complemented by extreme hard work.

Take an athlete for example. He will need to work hard on his training and fitness. But he will also need to work smart on his diet, his choice of coaches, the place and time of training and the equipment he will need. In this case working hard and smart are equally important in order for him to achieve his desired goal. The good thing about effort is that each of us are endowed with an unlimited reservoir and often times the only limitation is our own mind. The quantum of effort required for a task is directly proportional to the goal that needs to be achieved.

TEAM EXCELLENCE-IT'S A GROUP THING

I'm convinced that leadership is a hard thing. If we are honest, it is a tough job. Mainly because we don't get to choose who we work with. A team will comprise of people with diverse strengths, talents, aptitude, attitudes and temperaments. We know that no two people are the same. The skill of leadership in the pursuit of excellence is to be cognisant of that and yet not just deliver individual excellence but team excellence. The starting point is to ac*knowledge*, evaluate and appreciate the differences. You will need to assess individuals and then assign tasks based on each person's strengths. The worst thing you can do is to assign a person to a task that is completely not in their area of strength. They are bound to fail and to be discouraged, dissatisfied, burn out and maybe eventually resign. Worst of all it will affect productivity big time. So understanding a person's strengths is vital to a team's victory.

A common goal is a starting point. It is the leader's responsibility to effectively communicate the vision or goal in such a way that there is a transfer of ownership from an individual goal to a team goal. Studies indicate that when a team operates in a way that it wants to achieve the leader's goal rather than the team's goal, the team fails. And to add to it there's a lot of animosity and dissatisfaction.

On the other hand, when the leader has successfully articulated to his team not just the vision but has also transferred the ownership from himself to the team there is a higher chance of reaching the goal with success. Members of the team, once they own the goal, will realise that each of their inputs and participation will significantly affect the achieving of the said goal. It is important for the leader to eliminate favouritism and partiality. Dismantle operating by designations. The minute designations become the driving force behind a team walls are built up and the team will not deliver excellence. Care for each team member.

When individuals realise that they are cared for they will automatically go the extra mile. Your relationship shouldn't be just transactional. Develop a caring relationship. Lead by example. Team members follow the example set by the team leader or manager. If you as a leader go late to work, you can be sure that your team will follow suite. If you slack off be sure that your team will lack motivation. Never ask a team member to do something that you wouldn't do yourself. Celebrate interim wins. Reprimand based on facts and not perception. Reprimand privately and recognise effort publicly. Be firm but be kind. Review progress periodically.

Remember that what you tolerate is what you will get. If you tolerate mediocrity, mediocrity is what you will be left with. Push for excellence and you'll have a culture of excellence.

PROCRASTINATION- THE ENEMY OF EXCELLENCE

Greatest enemy to success or achievement isn't failure but procrastination. Success is about seizing the moment but when we procrastinate we are delaying and possibly destroying our chances to succeed. We often end up procrastinating because we might not have a goal in mind or the goal that we do have isn't a strong one. But a far more disturbing cause for procrastination is pure laziness. A popular proverb from the Bible brings out the dangers of laziness. It says "A hand of the diligent will rule while the slothful will be put to forced labour."

Procrastination will leave you devoid of purpose, strip you of future success, clothe you with mediocrity and open the gates to poverty. Procrastination is subtle but its consequences are irreparable and permanent. One way to avoid procrastination is to have a strong and fulfilling goal. This is not an option but is imperative. The thing about strong goals is that they develop passion and passion is the antidote to procrastination. Don't bite off more than you can chew. You should learn to manage your time well. Make a to do list and go through each item on the list systematically and enjoy checking them off as you complete each task. Do the difficult things early in the day that gives your mind better opportunities to think, analyse and respond. I find that relegating tough tasks to the evening or late night doesn't in any way aid productivity. It is very important to complete a task before you start a new one.

Multi-tasking is good but an unfinished task robs you of the joy of several finished tasks. Procrastination is an infectious and dangerous habit. Avoid hanging around with habitual procrastinators as the habit can spread. A useful tip to prevent procrastination is taking a 2-minute break during the day to realign your thoughts, clear your mind and refocus on the goal you have set for yourself.

TALENTS - THE CATALYST FOR EXCELLENCE

Each one is endowed with distinct talents and gifts. Talents range from the categories of art to literature, speaking to organising, baking to building, entrepreneurship to poetry and the list goes on. The fact of the matter is that everyone has a talent. A few may not have identified their talent yet and while a few others though aware of their talents may not have actively used them yet. For those who have discovered their talents and used them there is a great sense of satisfaction and fulfilment. I for one, discovered I had a talent for speaking and have used it to teach, encourage and uplift people by speaking from my life experiences. I get tremendous satisfaction when people from the audience have shared that what I spoke gave them hope and confidence during a particularly rough season in their life. I realise that in today's ultra-busy world where the pursuit of success occupies the highest time and mind share, the commodity which is getting scarce by the day is inspiration. No matter who you are and where you are, you definitely need inspiration and I believe that's the space that my talent of speaking words of encouragement and inspiration comes into play. There are a few guiding principles while using your talents that have changed my life.

- Utilise your talents to bless others not to promote yourself
- Humility is the soil on which the seeds of talents flourish
- There is no greater wastage than talents that are not used
- The more your talents are used the better they get
- Talent and effort go hand in hand

It's a grave error to assume that if you have talent you don't need to put in effort. I have found that the effort applied along with the talents possessed deliver the required results. For after all there are no short cuts to success.

Mental Push-Up for Today:

"One who is slack in his work is brother to one who destroys." – Proverbs 18:9

Write down in your own words the comparison that is made in this quote.

_____

_____

_____

Do people know you as someone who is excellent at what you do or someone who slacks off? Why?

_____

_____

_____

What are your personal challenges when you are striving for excellence in what you do? List them down!

_____

_____

_____

What practical steps will you take from now on to ensure you overcome these challenges?

_____

_____

_____

_____

Mental Push-Up for Today:

"The way we choose to spend time across a day will determine the outcome of our lives. Each minute that passes by, is either an opportunity seized or an opportunity lost!!"

In order of most to least, write down a list of things you spend time on through an average day.

_____

_____

_____

_____

Does this list tally with your list of personal priorities? If not, what can you change and how?

_____

_____

_____

_____

Watch out for opportunities that come your way today. Write down how you made the best of it.

_____

_____

_____

_____

_____

Mental Push-Up for Today:

"The challenge or obstacle isn't going to disappear just because you're avoiding it or procrastinating to take action. Face it now, do something about it and you will realise that it isn't such a big deal as you envisage it to be."

Is there a particular situation you have been struggling with to the extent that you avoid dealing with it at all? Describe it here.

_____

_____

_____

_____

_____

_____

List some action points that you can work on to tackle this situation that lies ahead of you. Put a deadline to these action points so that you ensure you get to it.

_____

_____

_____

_____

_____

_____

Mental Push-Up for Today:

"It's cooperation not competition that causes teams to function more efficiently on a long term sustainable basis."

Make a list of the teams you are a part of at work and other situations.

_____

_____

_____

_____

What are some of the challenges you face in your team(s)?

_____

_____

_____

_____

How can you overcome these challenges by applying the quote that you've read today?

_____

_____

_____

_____

_____

Mental Push-Up for Today:

"Don't kid yourself, your achievement will never be greater than your effort. Effort is the price you pay for achievement."

What do you understand from this thought?

_____

_____

_____

_____

What are some great achievements you hope to achieve in the next five years?

_____

_____

_____

_____

_____

What kind of efforts do you have to put in for these achievements to be realised?

_____

_____

_____

_____

_____

Mental Push-Up for Today:

"Talent is given to be used and not to be hidden. Put your God-given talent to work and watch it open doors of elevation."

Earlier in this workout series, you made a list of strengths that you have. Now, it is time to note your talents. Remember your talents are your innate abilities and gifts that God has given you. They are action words. Your strengths are your character traits that you can build on and hone. Know the difference!

Time to note your talents...even the hidden ones. Enlist them being completely immodest and honest.

_____

_____

_____

_____

_____

How many of these talents do you use at work and on a daily basis? If not all, how can you start using your unemployed gifts?

_____

_____

_____

_____

_____

_____

Mental Push-Up for Today:

"The emergence of success is primarily attributed to the convergence of desire, decision and discipline."

What are some achievements and successes you desire to see work out in the next one year? Write them down.

_____

_____

_____

_____

What decisions do you have to make to make these desires come to pass?

_____

_____

_____

_____

_____

What kind of discipline will be required on your part to keep up to these decisions so that your desire is fulfilled?

_____

_____

_____

_____

_____

Mental Push-Up for Today:

"If you aren't enjoying what you do, it is most likely because you aren't pursuing a goal that propels you forward. Goals are critical for progress."

Honesty Zone: What are some things that you do every day that you do not enjoy doing? Note them down here.

_____

_____

_____

_____

_____

_____

Analyse these things now. Do they tie in with some goals that you have? If not, why are you still doing them? If yes, are these goals really leading you towards your purpose? Write down your thoughts.

_____

_____

_____

_____

_____

_____

Mental Push-Up for Today:

"Success requires you to not go with the flow but to swim against the tide."

Are you someone who challenges existing norms and does things differently? If you believe so, write down why. If not, write down your reasons for that too!

_____

_____

_____

_____

_____

_____

_____

According to this quote, an important requirement of success is "going against the flow." How can you make this your reality?

_____

_____

_____

_____

_____

_____

_____

Mental Push-Up for Today:

"A common factor found among super achievers is belief. They never stop believing in their idea, skill, ability, talent or goal. They continue to believe despite discouragement, criticism and temporary setbacks. While talent and effort are certainly important; without the ability to believe, you certainly cannot achieve."

What is the key to becoming a 'super achiever' according to this thought?

_____

_____

_____

_____

How do you react to criticism and temporary setbacks? Describe your attitude in a nutshell.

_____

_____

_____

_____

How do you plan to keep yourself motivated to believe in yourself when things aren't going your way?

_____

_____

_____

_____

Mental Push-Up for Today:

"*Knowledge* is about being aware of the know how while wisdom is knowing and doing. Wisdom is the application of *knowledge*. *Knowledge* when not applied is futile."

What areas do you consider yourself *knowledge*able in? Don't be modest and note them down.

_____

_____

_____

_____

_____

_____

_____

Now, in all honesty, do you feel you apply this *knowledge* practically in situations that you are in? If yes, describe how. If not, how can you start applying it.

_____

_____

_____

_____

_____

_____

_____

Mental Push-Up for Today:

"Sacrifice is a key factor in the pursuit of success. You have to be willing to let go in order to gain."

Identify things in your life that stand in the way of achieving what you want to. Make note of them here.

_____

_____

_____

_____

_____

_____

How can you work on giving up these things over the next few weeks? Write down ways in which you can give these things up. These can be positive steps you can consciously work on taking in the days to come.

_____

_____

_____

_____

_____

_____

Mental Push-Up for Today:

"Wisdom is choosing not to do something that you will later regret."

Here's an exercise that will help you make wise choices. Note down below some choices you have to make in the next two to four weeks.

_____

_____

_____

_____

_____

_____

_____

Now for each of the choices, note the consequences of the decisions you will make. Weigh the importance of the decision based on the after-effects of the choice.

_____

_____

_____

_____

_____

_____

_____

_____

Mental Push-Up for Today:

"Greater awareness leads to greater confidence which in turn leads to greater growth opportunities."

Here's an exercise that will help you make wise choices. Note down below some choices you have to make in the next two to four weeks.

_____

_____

_____

_____

_____

_____

_____

Now for each of the choices, note the consequences of the decisions you will make. Weigh the importance of the decision based on the after-effects of the choice.

_____

_____

_____

_____

_____

_____

_____

_____

Mental Push-Up for Today:

"Knowing what to do and not doing it = Foolishness

Not knowing what to do and hence not doing it = Ignorance

Knowing and doing what's supposed to be done =Wisdom"

Make a detailed list below of the important things you know need to be done in the next few months. Now bookmark this page with a colourful post-it or sticker. Revisit this page every once in a while, to see how you're doing on your to-to list.

_____

_____

_____

_____

_____

_____

_____

_____

_____

_____

_____

_____

_____

Mental Push-Up for Today:

"Big things are achieved by doing the small things consistently and correctly."

What are some BIG goals you have set for yourself? Remind yourself of them by writing them below. Then against each goal, try to note at least three things you will.

_____

_____

_____

_____

_____

_____

_____

_____

_____

_____

_____

_____

_____

_____

_____

_____

_____

Mental Push-Up for Today:

"Opportunity definitely does knock but only on the doors of those who are prepared."

Have you missed some opportunities in the past because you were unprepared? If so, make note of them and write down how you could've prepared for them better.

_____

_____

_____

_____

_____

_____

_____

What can you do currently to prepare yourself so that you don't miss any breaks that come your way?

_____

_____

_____

_____

_____

_____

_____

Mental Push-Up for Today:

"Growth, satisfaction and pleasure are the outcome of doing that which you fear and which you consider to be difficult."

List some of the things that you fear and/or find difficult.

_____

_____

_____

_____

_____

_____

How can you overcome these fears and work your way ahead of them? Write down practical steps you plan to take to tackle each fear/difficulty on the list.

_____

_____

_____

_____

_____

_____

_____

_____

Mental Push-Up for Today:

"There is power in repetition, power to either build or destroy. A good thought, word or action when repeated builds and produces value, while the opposite when repeated erodes value and eventually destroys."

Make some habits that you have that you aren't pleased with and would like to change? Make a note of them below along with action steps on how you plan to work on getting rid of them.

_____

_____

_____

_____

_____

_____

What are some good habits you would like to form? How can you form them at the earliest?

_____

_____

_____

_____

_____

_____

_____

Mental Push-Up for Today:

"If you want it you got to be willing to work for it, nothing is going to fall into your lap."

How can you relate this thought to your life at present? Are there things that you need to 'work for?' Write about them below.

_____

_____

_____

_____

_____

_____

_____

_____

_____

_____

_____

_____

_____

_____

_____

Mental Push-Up for Today:

"To change outcomes, change your response to events that you face. Events that you experience are not controllable but your responses are."

How can you apply this thought to the situations that you are facing right now? What responses can you change to get different outcomes?

_____

_____

_____

_____

_____

_____

_____

_____

_____

_____

_____

_____

_____

_____

Mental Push-Up for Today:

"Being faithful and accountable with little is the door opener for bigger and larger responsibility."

What are some small responsibilities you have now? Note them below no matter how little they are.

_____

_____

_____

_____

_____

_____

_____

How can you be a better steward of these responsibilities?

_____

_____

_____

_____

_____

_____

_____

_____

EPILOGUE

So for the last six months I have become a regular member at the gym and I must confess up until then I had at best been irregularly regular. Now with a clear goal to increase my fitness levels and lose weight, it was imperative to make working out a daily habit. So for the first couple of months I got to do what I thought was right and self-instruct myself. I would do forty-five minutes on the treadmill and couple that with a few sets of the bench press. While this approach helped me marginally it wasn't substantial. So sixty days later I engaged a fitness coach who charted a day wise exercise regime which aims to work different sets of muscles through a variety of exercises. So each day there are different muscles which are assigned to be worked on such as back and biceps, chest and triceps and so on and so forth along with consistent work on the abs, shoulder and legs. The coach encourages me, pushes me and works on my weaknesses. At the end of four months I have made great progress. I feel more energetic and active, fat has been transformed to muscle and overall my fitness has gone to another level. All it needed was the conscious employing of a coach who was able to train and push me to step it up a notch and the results are visible.

You perhaps are pursuing wisdom. I'm guessing that's why you are holding this book right now. *Wisdom Workout* is your coach which will coach you daily to imbibe and apply wisdom in your situation, your environment and your context. *Wisdom Workout* will assist you to practice wisdom in the critical areas of purpose, relationships, communication, leadership and excellence. If I chose to ignore the advice of my coach in the gym or worse, never show up at the gym, I couldn't have experienced the fitness and health benefits that I now experience. I wish I had done this routine when I was twenty. But I am glad I have done it now even though it's twenty-one years later. So is the case with the *Wisdom Workout*. You will receive tremendous benefits if you access and apply these learnings daily and regularly. If you don't you may not make too much of progress. In fact, you may make no progress at all. Lastly it doesn't matter where you are in life today as long as you start the pursuit of wisdom now since its benefits last a lifetime. Above all, choose wisdom!